Racism in a Racial Democracy

Racism in a Racial Democracy

THE MAINTENANCE OF WHITE SUPREMACY IN BRAZIL

FRANCE WINDDANCE TWINE

Rutgers University Press

New Brunswick, New Jersey, and London

Fourth paperback printing, 2005

Library of Congress Cataloging-in-Publication Data

Twine, France Winddance
    Racism in a racial democracy : the maintenance of white supremacy
in Brazil / France Winddance Twine.
        p. cm.
    Includes bibliographical references and index.
    ISBN 0-8135-2364-8 (cloth : alk. paper). — ISBN 0-8135-2365-6
(pbk. : alk. paper)
        1. Blacks—Brazil—Social conditions. 2. Brazil—Race relations.
    3. Racism—Brazil. I. Title
    F2659.N4T86 1997
    305.896'081—dc21   97-10768
                                                                          CIP

British Cataloging-in-Publication data for this book are available from the British Library.

Manufactured in the United States of America

In honor of my maternal grandmother, Frances V. Lewis
*   (1897–1978), who gave me my dreams*
My mother, Mamie Lois Twine, who gave me life

In memory of my father, Paul Quinton Twine (1941–1994)

CONTENTS

ILLUSTRATIONS AND TABLES

Illustrations

Tables

ACKNOWLEDGMENTS

This book is dedicated to my maternal grandmother, Frances V. Lewis (1897–1978), my mother, Mamie Lois Phillips Twine, and my father, Paul Quinton Twine (1941–1994). My family's faith in the value of my work sustained me during a long and difficult process of research and writing. Win Warren generously provided financial support that enabled me to return to Brazil for a second research trip.

The completion of this book required the generosity and support of numerous friends, colleagues, and Brazilians who have all left their mark on it. I want to first thank all of the residents of the community I refer to as Vasalia who generously shared their lives and struggles with me. Several Brazilian families invited me into their homes and are now important members of my extended family. They gave me a home away from my field research and patiently tutored me in Brazilian Portuguese during my first months in Brazil. In this vein, I thank the families of Carla Barbosa de Brito, Fernando Neves, Regina Helena Vianna, Cesar Claudio Vianna, Antonio de Lourdes da Silva, Ana Lídia Vianna dos Santos Ivo, Lílian Janete Nunes de Meneze, Silvana Maria Martins Alves, and Cleonice Pankararu for their moral support, wonderful meals, and gracious tolerance of my never-ending questions about the dynamics of race in Brazil.

I also thank Imar Moreira, Luiz Barbosa, and Selma Oliviera. These Brazilian Americans supported me in numerous ways before, during, and after my field research by providing introductions and crucial contacts. It is doubtful that I would have completed this book without the support of Selma Oliviera. She accompanied me to Brazil for two weeks during my second fieldwork period and transcribed a portion of my taped interviews so that I could complete the first draft of this manuscript before assuming my teaching position at the University of Washington.

This book is based upon my dissertation research, which was directed by Professor Gerald Berreman at the University of California at Berkeley. I benefited greatly from working with such a humane mentor. My dissertation committee constituted what I refer to as my "dream team" of anthropologists and sociologists: Margaret Conkey, Kristin Luker, Troy Duster, Pedro Noguera, and Nancy Scheper-Hughes.

During the past two years I have been grateful to my colleagues in the Women Studies Department at the University of Washington in Seattle for providing me with a feminist milieu in which to teach and work. I especially wish to thank Susan Jeffords and Shirley Yee, consecutive directors of Women Studies for granting me release time from teaching during the final stages of manuscript preparation. Professors Tani Barlow and Sue-Ellen Jacobs supported this project by generously sharing material and pointing me to various journal articles and books that bore directly upon some aspect of my research.

Naheed Islam, Rebecca Aanerud, Caroline Chung Simpson, Priscilla Wald, Katharyne Mitchell, Julia O'Connell Davidson, and Judith Howard read and offered insightful comments about various portions of drafts of this book. My research assistant, Lara Harris, gave me constant support by locating and obtaining references at the last minute.

I owe a debt of gratitude that I can never repay to Louisa Schein, my colleague at Rutgers University, for introducing me to Martha Heller, the Social Sciences Editor at Rutgers University Press. I could not have asked for a more passionate and supportive editor. During the review process, her comments, along with those of Ellen Basso and Howard Winant, were invaluable in guiding me through the final stages of manuscript preparation. I am especially thankful to the Departments of Anthropology at Princeton University and the University of California at Santa Cruz for inviting me to present sections of this book in draft. Special thanks to Carolyn Martin Shaw.

Several institutions supplied funding at various stages of the research and writing. The University of California at Berkeley awarded me a Graduate Research Fellowship, which funded my first research period in Brazil. In 1993–94 I wrote the first draft of this manuscript while receiving a dissertation grant from Colorado College in Colorado Springs. I thank the anthropology and sociology departments at Colorado College for providing me with a home and thank the following community of scholars for their friendship and intellectual stimulation: Michael Siddoway (mathematics), Tom McGlinn (physics), and Margi Duncombe, Jeff Livesay, and Katarina Wegar (sociology). The Boeing Faculty Assistance Grant at the University of Washington gave me funding to revise the manuscript during the summers of 1994 and 1995.

Ara Wilson, Charm Farris Stephens, Michael Siddoway, and my uncle, Jim Pertle, have given me various forms of intellectual, moral, and practical support over the past decades. I am especially grateful for all the support that they gave me during my field research in Brazil. I am blessed to have a group of friends to catch me in the midst of fatigue fogs generated by demanding work. In this vein I thank the following friends for their support: Tom McGlinn, Naheed Islam and Raihan Zamil, Pedro Noguera and Patricia Vattoune, Tony de Falco, Darrell Robinson, Arnell Hinkle and John Wolfe, Maria Franklin, and Tim Riera.

I am particularly thankful for the enthusiasm of my partner of eight years, Jonathan Warren, who consistently encouraged me when I had no research funding and no secure employment. Jonathan Warren, a sociologist, accompanied me to the field on two occasions and supported me during all phases of my research and writing. In addition to assuming virtually all of the responsibilities for running our household, he read, commented upon, and reread every chapter of this book. I have benefited from his generosity as a scholar and a friend.

San Francisco
November 1996

Racism in a Racial Democracy

CHAPTER 1

Introduction

Anthropology has in the century played an important role in Brazilian society. It described and brought to public attention those aspects of Brazilian life which were, in the past, a source of embarrassment. . . . Along with writers of fiction, anthropologists have helped Brazilians to discover themselves.
—Charles Wagley (1979, 9)

Any study of racism in Brazil must begin by reflecting on the very fact that racism is a taboo subject in Brazil. Brazilians imagine themselves as inhabiting an anti-racist nation, a "racial democracy." This is one of the sources of their pride and, at the same time, conclusive proof of their status as a civilized nation.
—Antonio Sérgio Alfredo Guimarães (1995, 208)

On 13 May 1996, the anniversary of the abolition of slavery in Brazil, six black students at Brazil's most prestigious public university planted an eight-foot wooden cross on the main lawn of the University of São Paulo. On this cross they strapped a black man whose scores had not earned him entry into this state-subsidized university. The students have continued this action on the 13th of each subsequent month in their campaign for the establishment of a system of quotas that would ensure that a minimum number of Afro-Brazilians and people of color be admitted to the university. Although at least 45 percent of the Brazilian population is estimated to be black and mixed-race, only 1 percent of the student body at the University of São Paulo is nonwhite. The students are demanding that 10 percent of the slots in the opening class be reserved for Afro-Brazilian students. This act was described in the U.S. press as "a vivid demonstration of how the terms of racial debate are changing in Brazil."[1]

The leader of this nascent campus affirmative action movement is

Fernando Conceição, a thirty-five-year-old student, who was inspired to fight for racial diversity after spending a year in the United States on a Fulbright fellowship. Conceição identified U.S. black struggles for equality as the inspiration for his own struggle to increase Afro-Brazilian access to higher education. He is quoted in the *Wall Street Journal* as arguing that "you have a black middle-class [in the United States] because blacks are willing to fight." In this same article, Roberto Campos, a white Brazilian congressman, claims that "Brazilian whites lack a sense of guilt about the past mistreatment of blacks that motivated many white Americans to support affirmative action."

What is striking about this incident is not the protest, but its small size and the general lack of support that it is receiving thus far from Afro-Brazilians and other nonwhites. Remarkably, protests like the one described above continue to be highly marginal and led by the rare black Brazilian who has spent time studying abroad. Imagine for a moment that the African American population in the United States was 45 percent instead of 12 percent of the general population. If the black university population were only 1 percent, one would expect a movement of this type to generate support among blacks across class. In contrast, at least up to now, antiracist activists have not been successful in generating even minimal support among nonelite Afro-Brazilians for antiracist programs.

Working-class Afro-Brazilians have been notably absent among antiracist activists and organizers. With a few exceptions such as congressional representative Benedita da Silva, the struggle against racism has involved a minority of middle-class Afro-Brazilian professionals. John Burdick has characterized the movement in this way.

> The black movement is currently far from being the mass political phenomenon to which its militants aspire. . . . Even optimistic observers concede the movement has a fairly narrow social base . . . estimated to have only about 25,000 active followers, out of an Afro-Brazilian population that the movement estimates at over 70 million. . . . Black consciousness groups are composed primarily of professionals, intellectuals and upwardly mobile students, a pattern that has characterized the movement from the start. (1995, 177)

Numerous scholars have commented upon the failure of educated antiracist activists to generate support for a collective antiracist movement among nonwhites in Brazil. For example, Rosana Heringer concludes that "what is clear about the Black movement's message of racial, social, and economic inequality is that it has not created a common identity or cause among the majority of non-Whites" (1996, 205)

Theoretical Concerns: Common Sense

If the antiracist movement in Brazil hopes to succeed in generating broad-based support, then what Stuart Hall refers to as a "sort of racist common sense" must be challenged and transformed. Drawing from the work of Antonio Gramsci, Hall aptly summarizes the importance of common sense when considering how to strategically intervene into racist ideologies. This has relevance for debates about racial hegemony in Brazil.

> Why, then is common sense so important? Because it is the terrain of conceptions and categories on which the practical consciousness of the masses of people is actually formed. It is the already formed and "taken for granted" terrain, on which more coherent ideologies and philosophies must contend for mastery; the ground which new conceptions of the world must take into account, contest and transform, if they are to shape the conceptions of the world of the masses and in that way become historically effective. (1986, 21)

If Brazilians are to transform their nation into a real *democracia racial* (racial democracy), then a nuanced analysis of the conceptualization and negotiation of everyday racism among nonelites is required.

On 5 January 1989, President José Sarney signed into law Lei N° 7.716, which, for the first time in Brazilian history, defined crimes that result from prejudice against race or color as felonies. The law became part of the new Brazilian Federal Constitution and included articles that criminalized denial of access on the basis of color or race to services in public locations such as bars, restaurants, hotels, and sporting clubs, and to admission to private or public educational facilities. This law was a consequence of the efforts of the *movimento negro* (black movement). According to Brazilian sociologist Antonio Sérgio Alfredo Guimarães, "To this date nobody has been sentenced on a racist charge" (1996) Echoing this sentiment, Heringer notes that "missing is a sense that racial discrimination in Brazil is more than isolated actions of individuals. In this context, Black movement organizations have recognized that their main legal defense at the time of the 1988 Constitution—the codification of racism as a crime—has not produced the positive anti-racist effects they envisioned" (1996, 205)

An extensive body of literature on social and racial inequalities in Brazil has documented pervasive disparities by color and race, particularly in the post–World War II period. Anthropologists, historians, sociologists, and political scientists have analyzed and measured racial disparities in many spheres of Brazilian life including the following: labor market participation and income (Hasenbalg 1983; Silva 1985; Webster and Dwyer 1988; Wood 1988; Lovell 1989; Silva and Hasenbalg 1992; Castro and Guimarães 1993), social relations (Harris 1952; Hutchinson 1952), social mobility (Azevedo 1951; Bastide and Fernandes 1955; Cardoso and Ianni 1960; Fernandes 1969; Andrews 1991), racial attitudes (Willems 1949; Degler 1971) literacy and education (Cunha 1987; Pinto 1987; Figueira 1990; Hasenbalg and Silva 1990; Rosemberg 1990); language (Gilliam 1988); interracial marriage (Lowrie 1939; Silva 1987; Telles 1993; Twine 1996) immigration policies (Skidmore [1974] 1993; Meade and Pirio 1988); folklore (Carvalho-Neto 1978); spatial and residential segregation by skin color (Pierson 1942; Rosemberg 1990; Telles 1992); media representations and popular culture (Carvalho-Neto 1978; Simpson 1993), and infant mortality rates (Lovell 1987).

The central concern of this book is with this paradox of pervasive racial inequality and the continued failure of antiracist organizations and antiracist policies to generate grassroots support among nonelites for antiracist programs. Michael Hanchard, a political scientist, begins his study of the Afro-Brazilian antiracist activist movement in Brazil with this question:

> Why has there been no sustained Afro-Brazilian social movement in Brazil comparable to the Civil Rights Movement in the United States or nationalist insurgencies in sub-Saharan Africa and parts of the New World during the post–World War II period? Even though there have been attempts great and small to coalesce a divergent array of people into a racially based movement for social change during this period, there has been no national movement within civil society against racial inequalities and subordinations in Brazil. (1994, 5)

Sharing Hanchard's concern, I present an empirical study that will address this question from the perspective of ordinary Brazilians who are not engaged in antiracist activism. Previous studies by historians, sociologists, and political scientists have sought an answer to this paradox by analyzing the elite (Skidmore [1974] 1993), the state (Hasenbalg 1979), or antiracist activists (Hanchard 1994). My aim is to provide an ethnographic study of the discursive and material practices of the *povão* (the people), the nonelites. In a 1992 historical review of the social science literature on race relations in Brazil, Howard Winant concludes that

> despite its considerable strengths, the literature on race in Brazil suffers from a series of debilitating problems, including a neglect of the discursive and cultural dimensions of racism, an exaggerated belief in the omnipotence of elites where racial management is concerned, and a tendency to downplay the tensions and conflicts involved in Brazilian racial dynamics. The limitations derived from a deep-seated tradition of class-reductionism, which is manifest in the classic studies of the early post-war period (the revisionists), but latent even in the more recent work of the (structuralists). (1992, 192)

In the preface to the 1993 reprint of his book *Black into White: Race and Nationality in Brazilian Thought*, Thomas Skidmore argues for the necessity of an analysis of nonelites:

> But what about the rest of the millions of Brazilians? We are only beginning to gain insight into the world according to the "nonelites." . . . Research on popular attitudes such as race and national identity offer an essential and enlightening counterpoint to my focus on elite thought and behavior. In the fourteen years since this book was first published, relatively little new research on the themes defined here, especially the link between race and nationality. This can perhaps best be explained by the fact that Brazilian scholars, especially from the established academic institutions, continue for the most part to avoid the subject of race, in virtually all of its aspects, at least in the twentieth century. ([1974] 1993, xi)

I seek to complement the work of previous scholars of Brazilian racial inequality by bringing to the center of analysis the practices and voices of nonelite Brazilians. I present here a narrowly focused ethnography of everyday discursive and material practices that leave white supremacy intact. In other words, I am concerned with how ordinary Brazilians perceive, conceptualize, and negotiate multiple forms of racism in order to expand theoretical understandings of racial hegemony in contemporary Brazil. My aim is to illuminate why nonelite Brazilians, particularly Afro-Brazilians, continue to have faith in the Brazilian racial democracy.

The Racial Democracy Myth

In 1933 Gilberto Freyre, a social historian, published *Casa Grande e Senzala*.[2] The publication of this book signaled the birth of the Brazilian democracy's racial myth. Freyre provided a sanitized version of Brazil's long history of colonization and slavery. The devastating effects of this ideology for antiracist organizing today are described by Carlos Hasenbalg:

> By stressing the positive contributions of Africans and Amerindians to Brazilian culture he subverted the racist assumptions of contemporary social analysts such as Oliviera Vianna. At the same time, Freyre created the most formidable ideological weapon against antiracist activists. His emphasis upon the plastic character of the Portuguese colonizers cultural background and the widespread miscegenation among the Brazilian population led him to the notion of a racial democracy. (1985, 25)

Skidmore offers an analysis of how the Brazilian elites formulated a national project to "whiten" the "racial stock" of Brazil while simultaneously generating an arena of moral superiority in comparison to countries like the United States.

> While still believing that white is better and that Brazil was getting whiter, elite spokesmen after 1930 gained further satisfaction and confidence from the new scientific consensus that black was not inherently worse and thus that the racist claim that miscegenation must result in degeneration was nonsense. For approximately two decades after 1930, this Brazilian satisfaction at the discrediting of scientific racism led to the argument that Brazilians' alleged lack of discrimi-

nation made them morally superior to the technologically more advanced countries, where systematic repression of racial minorities was still practiced. The United States was the favorite example; Nazi Germany became another. (1990, 27)

In August 1943, U.S. black sociologist E. Franklin Frazier published an assessment of the position of Afro-Brazilians. In his analysis of the situation, Frazier provides the U.S. reader with one of the central tenets of the Brazilian racial democracy myth:

Namely in Brazil there is no stigma attached to Negro blood. "One drop of Negro blood" does not make a person Negro and condemn him to become a member of a lower caste. . . . Moreover it is generally accepted as an unexpressed national policy that the Negro is to be absorbed into the total population. It was with this in mind that a Brazilian statesman reminded [President] Roosevelt that in a hundred years Brazil would have no Negroes whereas the U.S. would have the problem of twenty or thirty million.[3]

In the post–World War II period, the United Nations Educational, Scientific, and Cultural Organization (UNESCO) funded a group of social scientists to conduct research on race relations in Brazil, a nation then considered to be a model of racial democracy. The funding generated a rich body of ethnographies published in the 1950s and 1960s that debunked the myth that Brazil was such a democracy.[4] However, while recognizing racial inequalities, scholars tended to stress socioeconomic status as the primary axis of power and deemphasized color and race as an axis of inequality. This deemphasis of race as an axis of power and faith in Brazil's racial democracy is illustrated by Charles Wagley's introduction to a volume published in 1952 entitled *Race and Class in Rural Brazil*. Wagley argues that "Brazil is renowned in the world for its racial democracy. Throughout its enormous area of a half continent race prejudice and discrimination are subdued as compared to the situation in many countries. . . . Today it may be said that Brazil has no 'race problem' in the same sense that it exists in other parts of the world; people of three racial stocks, live in what are essentially peaceful relations" (1952, 7).

In the 1970s, academics began to reconceptualize the meaning of racism in Brazil. Critiquing the body of literature produced by U.S. scholars and journalists, Guimarães argues that

> Anglo-American elite anti-racism was a no less active participant in the mystification and idealization of Brazil as a racial paradise. . . . Perceptions began to change only when Civil Rights laws were enacted in the United States. Only then could unequal racial opportunities be seen clearly operating and reproducing themselves through social mechanisms—schooling, unemployment, historic poverty, and urban de facto segregation. The changing perceptions of racial discrimination in the United States influenced both the Anglo-American perception of Brazil and the agenda of Western anti-racism. Thereafter, the identification of structural racial inequalities disguised in class or status terms became an important issue. Brazilian and North American racism had become much more alike. (1995, 210–211)

Despite a body of social science literature documenting racism, this mythology of the Brazilian racial democracy is still embraced and defended by nonelite Brazilians. Scholars have argued that the continued faith of nonelites in racial democracy is a primary obstacle to the development of a sustained and vital antiracist movement in Brazil. For example, Hasenbalg described this ideology of racial democracy as "the most powerful integrative symbol created to demobilize blacks and legitimate the racial inequalities prevailing since the end of slavery" (1979). Abdias do Nascimento, one of the first Afro-Brazilian antiracist public intellectuals elected to the Brazilian National Congress, argues that: "Thus the black movement expands enormous energies trying to convince its own people that their situation is due to racial discrimination. Continuously we must ask the question, 'Does racism really exist in Brazil?,' turning our energies away from the real questions facing us in [this] struggle" (1979).

To date, community studies of Brazilian race relations have not examined this continued faith of nonelites, particularly Afro-Brazilians, in the racial democracy. Previous studies have also tended to take for granted the meaning of racism rather than asking what constitutes acts of racism and antiracism for ordinary Brazilians. The preservation of a white supremacist racial order in a political democracy must consider the actions of Afro-

Brazilians. I agree with the historian George Reid Andrews who, in his assessment of the literature on race in Brazil, has argued that "surprisingly little attention is paid to the role of the subordinate racial groups, perhaps on the grounds that it is the whites who create and maintain racial hierarchy. But as a rich and growing historical literature makes clear, the dominated always participate in that process of creating and not just as helpless victims and objects. Even when they act from a position of weakness and disadvantage, their actions and decisions play a central role in determining the course of historical change" (1991, 15). In this book, I assume that while constrained by structural and institutional forms of racism, nonelites, particularly Afro-Brazilians, are not passive victims of the state. I ask how Afro-Brazilians in a political democracy cope with racism in ways that tend to preserve racial inequalities.

Passing as an American Anthropologist: Race, Class, and Gender in the Field

As a light–brown-skinned U.S. woman who was socially classified as a *mulatta* within Brazil, I was positioned very differently from white and nonblack researchers. My research topic, combined with my race, gender, and nationality, generated ambivalence for local residents, many of whom could not distinguish me from native Brazilians. It was often assumed, particularly by nonelites (who typically had never known a U.S. black), that I spoke Portuguese with an American accent because I had lived in the United States for a long time. They questioned whether I was really a North American, whether I had really been born in the United States, preferring instead to think that I was "passing" as an American. My authenticity as a U.S. researcher was repeatedly challenged by working-class Afro-Brazilians, who suspected me of trying to obtain better treatment from the white elites by presenting myself as a foreigner.

Angela Gilliam, a black U.S. feminist anthropologist, has described a situation that echoes what I encountered as a black female researcher: "Everyday I received startling inputs that affected me in much the same way as do those quasi-blinding strobe light shows mixed with white electronic music. It took a while to muster up my conscious forces. I already knew that as a black person leaving this country that my so-called status automatically changed, but I wasn't prepared for my looking and seeming so Brazilian that I would be accused of trying to 'pass as a foreigner'" (1992).

I had found no discussion in the feminist and nonfeminist literature on self and subjectivity in field research to prepare me for the racism and sexism that I encountered as a U.S. black feminist researcher in Brazil (Landes 1970).[5] Thus, I was not prepared for the high degree of hostility that I often encountered among some Brazilians when I attempted to engage them in a discussion of racial inequality in Brazil. To my surprise, I found that white elites were more comfortable discussing this topic with me than some Afro-Brazilians and other people of color.

While my U.S. nationality and class privilege enabled me to demand a certain degree of respect and sometimes protected me from vulgar forms of racism, it also generated social distance between me and some Afro-Brazilians (primarily light-skinned mulattas) who resented the preferential treatment that I received in comparison to them because of my status as a non-Brazilian. The privileges that my nationality, education, and class afforded and my routine violation of traditional gender roles generated discomfort and hostility among the Afro-Brazilians, with whom I had hoped to establish cordial relationships.

Like other women researchers, I found that my ability to conduct my research was contingent upon my being accepted as a "respectable" member of the community (Powdermaker 1939; Landes 1970). This respect required someone to "authorize" me. Friendships with two women, whom I call Ariana and Moema, were critical in sanctioning me, thus providing me with access to a range of socially segregated communities. These women, both schoolteachers, became my closest allies and supporters. They helped me collect the data for this study by integrating me into their familial, social, and professional networks.

Moema, a thirty-two-year-old white teacher, was my constant companion. As an unmarried elite woman with no children, no husband, and a servant to do her cooking and cleaning, Moema had a degree of leisure and autonomy unusual for women of any class background in Vasalia. As the granddaughter of Italian and Portuguese plantation owners, she had social ties to the white elite and introduced me to key members of the community who eventually granted private interviews on the topic of racism. Although Moema did not initially believe that my topic merited much attention, she smoothed my path in various ways and convinced members of the Euro-Brazilian elite that it was in their interest to discuss these issues with me or my partner.

Moema introduced me to her colleague Ariana when I expressed interest in meeting *black* professionals, who, given their small numbers, are difficult to encounter. She described Ariana as the daughter of the "wealthiest" black in the community. In contrast to Moema, Ariana was a married woman and the mother of a six-year-old daughter, so she lacked freedom of movement and racial privilege. Despite her busy schedule, Ariana spent hours talking to me in her kitchen and telling me her struggles as an outsider in this community. I developed the strongest bond with Ariana, because, as an educated black Brazilian (and outsider) in Vasalia, having moved there from a neighboring town after her marriage, she had a unique but neglected perspective on Brazilian racial dynamics.

There is a compelling body of quantitative research and macroanalyses of the material conditions of life for Afro-Brazilians and nonwhites in Brazil. However, there are virtually no book-length studies available in English with analyses of racism that center the voices of Afro-Brazilians. This book provides a microcultural analysis of racism that highlights the practices of working- and middle-class Afro-Brazilians and Euro-Brazilians morally opposed to racism.

The Outline of the Book

This book is based on ten months of research that I conducted during two separate periods between January 1992 and February 1994. During that time, I lived with a working-class Afro-Brazilian family. With the assistance of Jonathan Warren I conducted fifty-three focused live history interviews to supplement participant observation and household surveys.

The book incorporates the voices of Afro- and Euro-Brazilians who occupy a range of age, color, gender, and occupational positions. I am particularly concerned with how Afro-Brazilians manage the contradictions and the gap between their idealized image of Brazil as a racial democracy and the realities of everyday racism. In the chapters that follow, I explore practices and interpretive frameworks that reproduce white supremacist ideologies and structures. These discursive and material practices help Afro-Brazilians sustain a sense of hope and dignity as they cope with pervasive racial inequalities.

Chapter 2 situates the research site, the town of Vasalia, within the larger region. After giving a brief history of the community's establishment, I discuss recent shifts in the political economy of this town, located on a former coffee plantation. I introduce the reader to the working-class family that adopted me during my ten months of residence.

Chapter 3 outlines the ideological terrain of *commonsense* understandings of racism. It asks what constitutes an act of racism in Vasalia and identifies which forms of racism are not accounted for in the definitions of racism that Vasalians provided. I identify a disjuncture between the measures Vasalians use when considering racism and the more expansive criteria used by previous researchers of racial inequality in Brazil.

Chapter 4 explores how Brazilians defend their faith in the *racial democracy* when they are challenged to explain the absence of a black elite and the dominance of whites in virtually all positions of power and prestige. I provide a typology of the explanations or discourses employed by Vasalains when I call attention to the *whiteness* of the elite. I then analyze this repertoire of discursive defenses that attempts to restore the invisibility of white supremacy in Vasalia, thus avoiding a recognition of racial inequality.

Chapters 5, 6, and 7 examine practices that, instead of directly or effectively challenging white supremacy, perpetuate it. Chapter 5 analyzes the Brazilian national discourse of *mestiçagem* (race mixture) and the practice of *embranquecimento* (whitening) among Vasalians. I begin by analyzing the dominant aesthetic hierarchies that emerged in private and public conversations. These illuminate and underscore how Vasalians articulate and embrace aesthetic ideals that valorize European ancestry while denigrating physical traits that signify African ancestry. After documenting the predominance of a white supremacist aesthetic hierarchy, I consider Euro-Brazilian resistance to mestiçagem.

Chapter 6 examines memory and memorializing practices. I explore how Vasalians construct and strategically whiten family genealogies, family memorabilia, and narratives of local history. Practices that serve to whiten the genealogies of the body of the nation, the town, and their families sustain white supremacy. Beginning with a discussion of white inflation as it is articulated in the federal census, this chapter examines registration practices that artificially inflate the number of whites that appear in federal records.

Afro- and Euro-Brazilians in Vasalia routinely whiten their "official" selves and their families. Then I explore the repetitive omission of African-descent relatives motivated by what I refer to as "willful forgetting" or dis-remembering in family histories. I analyze this practice of willful forgetting as articulated in public and private spheres.

Chapter 7 provides an analysis of how Afro-Brazilian professionals respond to acts that they consider racist. This chapter explores the efficacy of common Afro-Brazilian responses to the racism that they encounter in their professional and social lives. I argue that the strategies employed to manage racism, while effective in maintaining cordial relations between upwardly mobile middle-class Afro-Brazilians and white elites, fail to effectively challenge white supremacy. I conclude with a discussion of the consequence of this for children, particularly Afro-Brazilian children. Lacking an arena in either the private or public sphere to explicitly discuss racism, children do not gain access to antiracist discourses or practices.

CHAPTER 2

Vasalia:
The Research Site

*I*n 1991 Brazil had a population of 146.1 million, the sixth largest in the world after China, India, the United States, Indonesia, and the Russian Federation. Brazil, encompassing 3,286,470 square miles, is the largest country in South America. Occupying 47.3 percent of the continent, Brazil shares borders with ten countries. Chile and Ecuador are the only countries in continental South America that don't share a border with Brazil (Fundação Instituto Brasileiro de Geografia e Estatística—IBGE 1994).

The Federal Republic of Brazil is comprised of twenty-six states and a federal district. These states are divided into five major regions: the North, Northeast, Southeast, South, and West Central. The states of São Paulo, Minas Gerais, Rio de Janeiro, and Espirito Santo comprise the Southeast region.[1] São Paulo, Minas Gerais, and Rio de Janeiro, respectively, are the three most populous states in Brazil. In 1990, Rio de Janeiro, third in population size, had a population of 12.5 million.

Vasalia

I am carefully unpacking the "Holy Trinity," the combination of black, red, and white pepper that my Creole grandmother Frances considered the essential spice in Louisiana cooking. As I set the African red pepper on the kitchen table in an effort to transform a small part of the space into my own,

FIGURE 1. The main street of Vasalia. The bank, post office, cabaret, public secondary school, and Catholic church are located on this main artery. The banner announces The Festival in the Mountains, an event sponsored by the Village Club. *(Photo by the author.)*

Dona Rosaria tells me (and three of her daughters) that this pepper is going to ruin my health. They continue with warnings that only *bahianos* (residents of Salvador, Bahia), not *brasileiros mesmos* (real Brazilians) eat hot peppers. Months later, that pepper will come to symbolize the heated arguments and the disruption that I will bring to my host family. Now I am perplexed by their negative response to my pepper. I learn that brasileiros mesmos associate pepper and hot flavors with Africa, and most importantly with bahianos, whom they don't consider real Brazilians because they retain too many African cultural traits. They say that real Brazilians are cultural hybrids.

Vasalia[2] is a small town located in a coffee-growing region in Rio's northwestern interior. In 1879 Vasalia was officially recognized and established as a district of the municipality of a city I refer to as Boa Vista. According to local records,[3] Boa Vista was formally recognized as a municipality in the 1870s. Prior to this time, the area had been closed to settlement by the colonial government in an effort to control the flow of precious metals out of the state of Minas Gerais.

Brazil is the world's largest producer and exporter of coffee. The largest coffee plantation in Vasalia was established in the 1860s by an Italian who immigrated to Brazil in the mid-1840s. Local residents reported that Italian immigrant plantation workers murdered the grandson of this Italian immigrant because he was brutal. The plantation he founded remains one of the biggest and most productive in the region, employing more than three hundred workers.

Vasalia is similar to several other small cities in this area in that it began as a coffee plantation, also served as a *rancho/venda* (mule stop) for *tropeiros* (transporters), and grew slowly into a small town. According to historian Stanley Stein, many towns in Rio de Janeiro once served as overnight transit stations: "The trading-station (venda) and its neighboring shelter (rancho) at which passing muleteers (tropeiros) could stop for the night and purchase corn for their animals and for themselves beans and *cachaça* (rum) fine and transparent like water and in taste resembling Scotch whiskey" ([1958] 1985, 5).

The folklore about the origins of the name of the town suggest that Vasalia had served as an important way station between the city of Campos and cities such as Belo Horizonte in Minas Gerais and towns in Espirito Santo. The original plantation around which Vasalia grew was probably a product of land settlement such as Stein describes:

> Another type of land occupation developed along the mule paths later opened in the higher areas of the municipio. Attracted by the lively market provided by the pack trains, squatters (*posseiros*) built ranches for tropeiros and their pack-animals and made small clearings for corn, beans, cane and pasture required by the trade. Some of these squatters subsequently obtained *seismarias* (land grants), others sold out to newcomers, and still others continued undisturbed in the occupation of considerable tracts of land. ([1958] 1985, 11)

Vasalia is under the political and economic control of approximately eight extended land-owning families of Italian and Portuguese origin who have intermarried. Based upon their town records kept in the private collections of an Italian-Brazilian family, a number of the Afro-Brazilian residents are the direct descendants of African slaves who were brought there to work in the gold mines of Minas Gerais. When the mines were exhausted, many of these blacks migrated to places like Vasalia in the states of Rio de Janeiro and São Paulo in search of employment opportunities.

Until January 1991, Vasalia was the district capital of the municipality of Boa Vista. Boa Vista was colonized relatively late for this part of Brazil because the region was part of a "forbidden zone." It had been placed off limits for settlement by the colonial government to control the flow of precious metals out of Minas Gerais. When the gold mines were exhausted and the mining industry began to collapse, the border region in the state of Rio de Janeiro was opened up for settlement and coffee production.

In 1992 I attended the 100th anniversary of the founding of the largest coffee plantation in this region. It had formerly operated with the forced labor of Indian and African slaves, and, after the abolition of slavery, the descendants of these same slaves and indentured Italian immigrants. Descendants of slaves and Italian immigrants still work there under conditions very similar to their ancestors'.

The workers with whom I spoke said that they are not paid wages, but are instead given housing, food supplies, and other in-kind services that make it difficult for them to accumulate sufficient capital to leave the plantation.[4] It is common for them to reach adulthood without completing even four years of primary education. Consequently, most agricultural workers are illiterate and have few skills that would enable them to leave a life of manual labor. Although there is a primary school building on the plantation and teachers are employed to teach the workers and their children, classes are offered on an irregular basis, as they are scheduled around the needs of coffee production.

I arrived in Vasalia in January 1992. According to the town residents and bibliographic research, this town has never been studied by a U.S. anthropologist. The deforestation of the region began in the late nineteenth century to make room for coffee production and it did not end until the 1970s. The naked hills of Vasalia and the surrounding area of northwestern Rio de Janeiro were once part of the Atlantic rainforest. Since the 1970s, there has been a dramatic change in the climate and elimination of most wildlife. This elimination, which includes birds, is dramatic even in comparison to urban areas in the western United States. The only birds that one sees are the caged ones that many residents keep in their windows during the day and that small business owners keep in front of their shops and storefronts.

TABLE 2.1   *Population of Vasalia, Census of 1991*

	Urban	Rural
Men	1,131	2,544
Women	1,184	2,268
Total	2,315	4,812

Source: Preliminary unpublished reports of Pedro da Silva Braga, Secretaria de Planejamento, Presidencia da Republica, Fundação Institution Brasileiro de Geografica e Estatistica.

The Demographic Context: Color and Race

In 1990, the population of Vasalia was reported to be 7,127 (see Table 2.1).[5] No published data with specific figures by color were available because until 1991 Vasalia was an administrative district of the municipality of Boa Vista and census data by color on Vasalia were combined with the other satellites of Boa Vista and published together as one figure. Moreover, during the 1960 and 1970 census no data on race/color were published by the federal government. Under military rule, questions related to color and race were eliminated from the national census.[6]

The 1980 census data, the most recent available figures by color, summarize the data for the six administrative districts of Boa Vista (see Table 2.2). According to these figures, *brancos* (whites) constitute 60 percent of the local population. We can assume that this figure is somewhat inflated, as Brazilians tend to claim a whiter identity on the basis of achieved characteristics such as education or income rather than color. (See Chapter 6 for a detailed discussion of the inflation of census numbers for whites.) According to the 1991 Brazilian census, the southern and southeastern regions contain the highest concentration of persons who self-identify as white (Fundação Instituto Brasileiro de Geografia e Estatística—IBGE 1995).

The Geography of Hierarchy: Spatial Segregation by Skin Color

There are two main streets with several secondary streets that feed into them. The homes of the plantation-owning families are all on those two streets

TABLE 2.2. *Population of Boa Vista (includes Vasalia), Census of 1980*

Categories in 1980	Men	Women	Total
Branca (White)	6,072	5,938	12,010
Parda (Brown)	2,548	2,399	4,947
Preta (Black)	1,486	1,288	2,774
Amarela (Yellow)	12	27	39
Sem declaração (Undeclared)	47	62	109

Note: Vasalia is one of six satellites of Boa Vista. Data from Boa Vista and its satellites are subsumed under these statistics.

or their arteries. The main entrance to the town is approximately 430 km (seven hours by bus) from the city of Rio de Janeiro. It runs into the main street of the town, which is named for a local plantation owner of Portuguese descent. Most of the streets carry the names of Italian and Portuguese plantation owners, state politicians, and military soldiers. There is a village country club, which consists of two swimming pools (a separate pool for children and adults), a playground, a sauna, and an enclosed game room with pool tables and a bar. A small eight-room hotel currently houses out-of-town construction workers. A coffee-processing center is on the right, near a new elementary school, a Brizola[7] school currently under construction, which will bring fifty new state jobs to the town.

As one proceeds, men and young boys can be seen riding horses (women don't usually ride horses) or walking. An occasional car will speed by, driven by a white middle-class man (and occasionally the wife or daughter of the rural land-owning elite). After about another 84 meters, a small valley and the main area of town come into view.

A church sits on the right side of the street as one enters the center of town. To the left of the church sits the original three-story plantation home, the oldest building in town. Several years ago, some residents waged a campaign to save this building from destruction. It has been abandoned for more than five decades and is dilapidated. Until about 1976, a movie theater was located across the street in view of the church. The theater was closed and torn down when residents began to buy televisions. Televisions did not become standard features in the homes of the vast majority of residents until the early 1980s.

On the opposite side of the street facing the church are the town homes of the oldest and wealthiest Euro-Brazilian *fazendeiros* (plantation owners) in the area. One home belongs to the Perreira family (Portuguese origin) and the other belongs to the Martinelli family (Italian origin). The Perreira family also owns a three-story home built in 1897, which is currently occupied by a family member in her late nineties. She lives in complete social seclusion and sees only a family servant who delivers a daily meal brought to her from her grandson's home next door.

Many of the elite families have dual residences in the large cities of Rio de Janeiro and Niteroi (an industrial city across the bay from Rio). The adult children of the Euro-Brazilian land-owning aristocracy provide their children with apartments when they send them to the federal universities in Rio or São Paulo to be educated. The majority of their male children have chosen to establish their primary residence and professions in these larger cities, while the daughters of these families tend to go and live for a period of six months to several years in Rio. If they don't marry a *carioca* (resident of the city of Rio de Janeiro), they usually return home and work as either schoolteachers or self-employed business owners. In several cases, women from middle-class and elite white families have gone to Rio, gotten married, gotten divorced, and then returned to marry a younger and poorer man from the community. These women are able to marry a second time after the age of thirty because they can offer land and wealth to their prospective husbands. There were several cases that involved divorced women or women more than thirty years of age who married men more than five years younger than themselves, which is considered scandalous in small rural towns.

There were no available maps of Vasalia, so I counted all of the buildings and residences on its four main arteries. On the principal street I counted one hundred residential structures, including apartment buildings, single-story, and two-story homes. Based upon interviews with residents, I identified only four families with an Afro-Brazilian head of household residing on the prestigious main street. Three of these families consist of Afro-Brazilian men and their Euro-Brazilian domestic partner. Only one family consisted of an Afro-Brazilian married to another Afro-Brazilian. In other words, three of the families were multiracial households that contained an Afro-Brazilian professional, their white wives, and their mixed-race children. The center of the town had a disproportionate number of Euro-Brazilian founding families of Italian and

FIGURE 2. The public television located in one of the poorest sections of Vasalia. It is turned on around 6:00 p.m. each night so that the residents can watch the *telenovelas* (soap operas) and *futebol* (soccer) on weekends. *(Photo by the author.)*

Portuguese descent. Afro-Brazilians were rarely seen walking or socializing on this street except when they did their grocery shopping or when they attended dances on Saturday night at the recently opened disco. Household censuses among these families suggest that a television is considered an essential piece of furniture, more valued than a refrigerator.

Walking downhill to the other side of town, only five minutes away, one enters a newer district and a very different neighborhood of poorer, darker-skinned individuals and recent migrants from the rural areas. This part of town was once the remaining holdings of a large coffee plantation owned by one of the wealthy Italian-Brazilian landowners. Approximately ten years ago, he sold his remaining holdings to the city and this neighborhood was established. The streets are cobblestoned, not paved, and a sign of the poverty of the residents is the public television located at the intersection of the two major streets that comprise this barrio. The television was purchased by the city several years ago so that residents who don't own a television could watch the *telenovelas* in the evenings and *futebol* (soccer) games on the weekends. A count of the houses in this section revealed a concentration of homes with two to three rooms, no indoor plumbing, few refrigerators, and *fogãos* (outdoor ovens). Afro-Brazilians, Euro-Brazilians, and mixed-race working-class and poor residents are concentrated in this recently built neighborhood, which is located downhill and out of sight of the more fashionable district of town where the white middle-class and rural elite have homes and businesses. The main artery of this neighborhood is where the most popular dance hall (among nonwhites) is located. It is open only on Saturday evenings.

Based on interviews and visual observation, more than 50 percent of the residents of this barrio are Afro-Brazilians and poor Euro-Brazilians, and the remainder are of mixed-race ancestry. This is where many of the barroom fights occur on weekends. A small brothel is also located here. Prostitution is said to have worsened and become a big problem in the town. During interviews (off tape), residents indicated that the majority are recent migrants from small farms or coffee plantation, referred to by the established town residents as the *zona rural*. Most residents have lived in town for less than three years. This barrio is evidence of the rapid expansion and population growth occurring in Vasalia. The expansion is partially due to the growth of the tomato industry. Until very recently (no one could provide a specific date), there was no *favela* (working-class or poor residential neighborhood) in this town. Now there is a very small one located at the (northern) back entrance to the town, with approximately forty families. Few of the residents of the old main street up the hill seem to know the residents of this district by name if they are not employed as their maids.

My Adoptive Family in Vasalia: Dona Rosaria

My entrée into Vasalia was a consequence of my relationship with Helena, an Afro-Brazilian with whom I had become acquainted in San Francisco. Helena immigrated to the United States as the *baba* (childcare worker) of a wealthy Euro-Brazilian family. I met her in 1991 at the Day of the Dead Parade in San Francisco. I told her that I was trying to identify a suitable small city in the state of Rio de Janeiro in which to conduct my research. She then suggested that I live with her family for several months since they always had extra room and were in need of additional income.

Helena left Vasalia at the age of sixteen to work as the *empregada domestica* (domestic servant) of a Brazilian soap opera actor in the city of

FIGURE 3. The Assembly of God Protestant church. *(Photo by the author.)*

Rio de Janeiro. Like many Afro-Brazilian women from poor families, she had begun working as a domestic servant for elite Euro-Brazilian families before she was twelve years of age. Helena told me that she had been sending a portion of her wages to her mother since she was thirteen to help support her family.

Dona Rosaria and her husband Joaquim are retired laborers in their sixties. They met when Dona Rosaria was fourteen years old. Prior to her marriage at sixteen, Dona Rosaria spent her childhood working as a field laborer on a coffee plantation. At the time of her retirement two years ago (1990), she had worked as a *cozinheira* (cook) at the public high school. Before that, she worked as a *lavandeira* (laundress) for approximately fifteen middle-class Euro-Brazilian families. A stroke that left the upper left side of her body paralyzed forced her to retire from her position as a cozinheira.

Joaquim, her husband, is also retired. Born and raised on a coffee plantation, he had spent his youth and much of his middle age working as an agricultural worker on coffee plantations owned by Italian-Brazilians. After working for years on coffee plantations, his most recent occupation had been as a road repair worker. As a retired employee of the city, he drew a comfortable pension. Neither Dona Rosaria nor her husband, Joaquim, had ever attended school. Thus, they were not literate although *all* of their thirteen surviving adult children are literate and well educated by Brazilian standards. Six of Dona Rosaria's adult children, five daughters and one son, had acquired vocational training and certification as primary or secondary school teachers and taught in the local community.

During my field research in Vasalia, my partner and I lived in a four-bedroom house with eight adults and two children. Five of these adults were the unmarried or separated children of Dona Rosaria and Senhor Joaquim. In addition to these five adult children, two grandchildren (a three-year-old and a one-month-old infant) and one son-in-law also lived with them. This home was purchased for US$6,000 in cash in 1986 by Helena, Dona Rosaria's daughter. Helena had accumulated savings during an eight-year period, working first as a live-in servant for an elite white Brazilian family living in the United States and later as a free-lance house cleaner.[8] We occupied a small bedroom that had been previously served as the kitchen before the house was remodeled and expanded.[9]

Dona Rosaria's family was the only Afro-Brazilian family living on a street dominated by the homes and businesses of white middle- and upper-class residents. Like most working-class Vasalians, they had no private telephone, car, or servant. However, because of the earnings of their adult children, including three who remained at home and worked as schoolteachers, they had what few working-class Vasalians have—disposable income that enabled the unmarried adult daughters to take vacations and spend money on luxury items such as designer eyewear and clothing. Dona Rosaria's family also received the equivalent of three monthly minimum salaries from their daughter Helena, a permanent resident of the United States.[10]

Some of the wealthiest members of the community live here. They own cars, live in spacious homes of eight to twelve rooms, and have many servants, including cozinheiras, babas, and empregadas domesticas. Another sign of the residents' wealth is the number of satellite dishes on this street. Of nine families, there were five satellite dishes,[11] which give them access to English-language, Spanish-language, and Portuguese-language programs originating in the United States and Mexico. Although I met no one in town who was fluent in English, the residents enjoy having access to U.S. cable stations. These residents also take several vacations per year on the coast, bringing servants with them. Typically, the male members of these families have studied or traveled abroad to the United States or Europe.

This is one of the main arteries in town and one of the few tree-lined streets. Several businesses are located here, including a hardware and supply store, a coffee warehouse, a factory for roasting coffee beans, a *botequim*,[12] and a toy store. This street is also unique in that it has a row of trees in the center. Several years ago, all of the trees on the main streets had been cut down. A woman climbed into the trees on this street and refused to leave until the city promised not to cut down the remaining ones.

With one exception, all of the neighbors were upper-middle-class Euro-Brazilian homeowners. I observed the high degree of social isolation and ostracism directed at Dona Rosaria's family during the ten months that I lived in their home. The social distance between them and their neighbors was a taboo subject that was never openly discussed in my presence. Nevertheless, I was aware that the members of the family rarely exchanged words with their neighbors and, aside from their next-door neighbor whose private telephone I occasionally used to receive calls once a month from the United States, they did not introduce me to any of their immediate neighbors.

Another example of the social distance between the Rosarias and their neighbors is that the Rosarias were never invited to enter their neighbors' homes during my field research period. In fact, the only nonwhites who I ever saw enter their neighbors' homes were servants and their adoptive black children who worked as unpaid servants.

The Economic Context: From Monocrop Coffee to Tomatoes

Like other regions of Brazil, this one is characterized by its reliance on a monocrop culture. Until four years ago, the economy of Vasalia was based almost entirely on coffee production. Although the town is also known for the wine that it produces, wine making does not provide many jobs and the wine is sold by only four Italo-Brazilian families to the local internal market. Also like other regions of Brazil, Vasalia has been vulnerable to a boom-and-bust cycle in relation to coffee production. When the price of coffee began to fall on the international market in the 1980s, farmers in small towns in the region began to consider growing other crops—crops less dependent upon an external (foreign) market. Around 1989, several farmers in the region began growing tomatoes.

Unlike coffee, which requires a large initial outlay of money for the purchase of equipment, a one-year growth cycle, and, until recently, a large permanent workforce, tomatoes require a much smaller initial capital outlay, a shorter growth cycle, and less intensive labor. Tomatoes need only a three-month growth cycle, so fewer workers are needed to reside full time on the coffee plantation. Moreover, tomatoes can be sold within Brazil to a more stable internal market. This created space for small farmers to survive if they could acquire land.[13]

When I arrived in Vasalia in January 1992, it was in the midst of a tomato boom. Trucks, loaded with tomatoes, were leaving three nights per week for the city of Niteroi. On Wednesday, Fridays, and Sundays the streets were full of men loading and preparing for the approximately seven-hour all-night drive to Rio. The expansion of the tomato industry brought a few men into the middle class. More jobs were created for independent truck transporters, storage facilities were needed, and men were needed to farm and load the trucks. During my first fieldwork period in 1992, construction began for a large warehouse for tomato storage and an outdoor market. A new neighborhood was carved out of the hills by bulldozers and construction of several houses was initiated.

Although the expansion of the tomato industry created more jobs for men, women did not benefit directly from it. Most of the job growth was occurring in the transportation and sales aspects of the industry, defined as men's jobs. The same underpaid farm laborers who had worked in the coffee industry could be used in the tomato industry. In fact, *less* labor is required for tomato production, so *fewer* seasonal jobs exist in this industry.

White Supremacy: The Racial Order in Vasalia

Afro-Brazilians are noticeably absent from all positions of power. Vasalia and the surrounding area had been colonized primarily by the Italians, Portuguese, and their African slaves. The Italians and Portuguese began arriving in the early 1840s, according to family trees and immigration documents that I examined in private family collections. Vasalians recognize the Portuguese and Italians as the colonizers and leaders in this region, with

FIGURE 4. The children of working-class families. Their mothers work primarily as empregadas domesticas for the middle-class families in town. *(Photo by Jonathan Warren.)*

the Italians being the predominant cultural influence. All of the important leadership positions are held by individuals who are descendants of the founding Italian or Portuguese families. Although several white women and black men ran for office, not a single nonwhite man was elected during the 1992 elections. The recently elected mayor and all nine of the city council representatives are white male descendants of Italian or Portuguese landowning families.

To illustrate how completely Euro-Brazilians dominate the socioeconomic, political, and religious life in Vasalia, I present a discussion that I had with Ariana, the *sole* second-generation dark-skinned Afro-Brazilian schoolteacher in Vasalia. Ariana describes herself as a preta and is the only dark-skinned Afro-Brazilian whom I met whose parents (whom she described as pretas) are both university educated. Her comments were typical of those of other Vasalians who are were unable to identify any Afro-Brazilians of wealth or status.

Ariana I have never seen a black priest, not even a moreno one.

FWT Never?

Ariana Never. Never, I really mean it, I never saw one (as a child). Maybe they exist. I'm sure [there must be a few]. . . . The first time I saw a black priest was in a soap opera. I have never seen a black priest in [real] life. People say that there are black priests . . . but most priests are whites.

FWT Why do you think there are few black priests? There are quite a few black Catholics living here.

Ariana . . . I think that [blacks] are discriminated against even in the church itself. So they don't advance. They might even get to the point where they are the priests' assistants, altar boys. But to be a priest, no. It's the Catholics themselves. I mean that people who follow the religion discriminate [against Afro-Brazilians]. So I think that generally it is the whites who are guiding, only the whites.

FWT Do you know any black ranchers in this region?

Ariana Rich ranchers? No. In this region, I don't know any black ranchers. I know negros who have some status [as small farmowners] But ranchers, plantation owners, no.

FWT No ranchers?

Ariana Not ranchers . . . all the ranchers are white. White. White. When I see someone with dark skin driving a car, he is the employee of a rancher.

The absence of black priests is just one example of the exclusion of Afro-Brazilians and nonwhites from all positions of authority. The exclusion of blacks from the priesthood, politics, business, and land ownership is not unique to Vasalia. Ronald Schneider has commented on the subordination of blacks and other nonwhites in Brazil.

Blacks in Brazil are much worse off in almost every way than whites. . . . This striking correlation of dark color with the lowest rungs of the socioeconomic ladder is manifest in all organizations. In Congress blacks are but 6 of 559, and the paucity of black or mulatto generals and admirals is matched by their absence from diplomatic service. The Catholic Church is equally unrepresentative, with only 5 black bishops out of some 370 and mere a 200 dark-skinned priests in over 14,000. Certainly the educational system contributes to these disparities, but there is much more at work in maintaining the low social mobility of blacks and mulattos and their exclusion form society's most vital institutions.(1991, 17)

I found this same pattern of Afro-Brazilian subordination and exclusion in Vasalia. Whenever I asked Vasalians to identify a black in a powerful position in their community, they would invariably name Pelé, the famous Brazilian soccer player, who is not from there. None could identify a person from the community. The one black medical doctor, Dr. Rudolpho, moved here to accept a position almost nine years ago.

Conclusion

Vasalia is an agricultural community dominated politically and economically by Euro-Brazilian families of Italian and Portuguese ancestry. Although historically dependent primarily on monocrop coffee production, the local economy is undergoing diversification with the recent introduction of tomatoes as a crop of choice. Some segments of the working class are experiencing mobility as they acquire jobs as independent truckers for the tomato industry, but there continue to be few options for women as these jobs are gendered.

I have also described one feature that Vasalia shares with Brazil at the national level—the virtual absence of dark-skinned Brazilians *and* Afro-Brazilians in the ranks of the elite. The religious, political, and economic elite is white dominated and male. In the following chapter, I shift attention to a discussion of Vasalian conceptualizations of racism.

CHAPTER 3

Mapping the Ideological Terrain of Racism

THE SOCIAL, SEXUAL, SOCIOECONOMIC, AND SEMIOTIC CONTOURS

Look, I can't even really explain to you what racism is. Thank God, because I don't practice it. I mean only a racist person can give you real examples of racist practices.
—Senhor Lorenzo, mayor of Vasalia

Racism ended about ten or fifteen years ago when I was thirty-one years old. But I can't give you any specific examples of racism. [Racism] is a feeling that one has around certain people.
—Luisa, Afro-Brazilian teacher

In my family, they would say, as everyone in Brazil says, there is no racism here. Everyone is equal . . . however, if you dated a black or if anyone in the family really loved a black person, the situation would change.
—Dr. Giovanni

What constitutes an act of racism? When asked to define it, Vasalians considered interracial social and sexual relations, while they typically failed to consider institutional racism, occupational segregation, electoral representation, media representations of blacks, and the distribution of power in their definitions of racism. As a U.S. black, operating with definitions of institutional racism generated by black activists during the civil rights movement, I anticipated more expansive definitions of racism than those I found in Vasalia.

In order to theorize about the meaning of racism in Vasalia, a nuanced analysis of everyday racism must begin with the question of "What constitutes an act of racism?" Do Brazilians use the same criteria as researchers and antiracist activists? Or do some Brazilians operate with a different set of criteria when defining racism? A number of scholars of racial inequality in Brazil have documented pervasive racism in Brazilian life (Wagley 1952; Hasenbalg 1985; Turner 1985; Cunha 1987; Pinto 1987; Figuera 1990; Lovell 1992; Silva and Hasenbalg 1992; Telles 1992; Warren 1997). However, the quantitative and qualitative research on contemporary forms of racism in Brazil has not explored the meaning of racism among nonelites and nonactivists. This chapter expands theoretical discussions of racism in Latin America by exploring the disjuncture between the common understandings of racism among Afro- and Euro-Brazilians and measures of racial inequality employed by researchers.

The chapter is divided into two sections. In the first section I outline the criteria used to define racism and the examples of racism that emerged in response to the question "What constitutes an act of racism?" In the second I analyze several forms of racism that are excluded from the predominant definitions of racism in this community. I discuss common forms of racism that have been measured by Brazilian scholars of racial inequality.

By identifying the disjuncture between the definitions of racism used by ordinary Brazilians and those used by researchers, I offer insight into why the *movimento negro* (black movement) has failed to generate grassroots support among nonelites in their campaign against racism. My research suggests that racial conflict can be minimized in a context of pervasive racial inequality precisely because commonsense definitions of racism may exclude more complex and covert forms of racism. I indicate potential sites of intervention for Brazilian antiracist activists attempting to mobilize grassroots support. If the definitions of racism held by some segments of the Afro-Brazilian community are more restricted than those used by antiracist activists and academics, then a viable antiracist movement will need to generate more expanded definitions of racism.

The Social Sphere

When asked to define racism, Vasalians typically begin by juxtaposing interracial social relations today with reference to the past, when racially

FIGURE 5. Dona Hilma, the owner of the public telephone in town, poses with her grandsons. *(Photo by Jonathan Warren.)*

based social segregation was enforced. This is seen in the definition of racism given by Jorge, a twenty-year-old Afro-Brazilian: "The plantation owners, who used to prohibit blacks from entering their homes. Blacks had to remain in the slave quarters. [Whites] didn't want to mix with them. . . . Blacks were not allowed inside of their houses, no! Blacks had to eat outside. Now, to-day, we don't have racism anymore because blacks can enter the kitchens and eat in the homes of whites."

This parallels descriptions of social relations between blacks and whites in Indianola, Mississippi, in the 1930s (Dollard 1937; Powdermaker 1939). Joaquim, the sixty-seven-year-old grandson of slaves and of a Portuguese plantation owner, described how much progress had occurred in this community by recalling the segregation of the public streets in the past. "There was a very straight row of trees. At the time, the poor people and people of color walked on one side and the white people on the other side. That is, the pretentious white people walked on the upper sidewalks of the street. Even

[at] the public festivals and dances, it was customary to remain segregated by color."

Tatiana, the fifty-one-year-old dark-skinned wife and homemaker of the only Afro-Brazilian family that lives on the fashionable main street of the town, describes this same pattern of formal (de facto) segregation that existed during most of the history of this community.

> Segregation ended. . . . It's been about twenty-five years, more or less. That is when it was all coming to an end. But at the club, where the people used to like to go, to the dances, . . . there was a club for whites and a separate club for blacks. Even if a black was someone like the father of Ariana, a lawyer, he still couldn't enter because he was black. Poor whites also weren't allowed to enter. Poor whites went to the blacks' dance, And also at the white dances, even if a black had money, he couldn't attend. If they were black they couldn't enter. And the main street was divided along racial/color lines. We were so accustomed to it that we didn't even get worked up about it. Even the stores where we did our shopping. The stores on the other side of the street, we didn't go there—one side was for whites and the other side was for blacks.

In their descriptions of Vasalia, the Brazilians interviewed contrasted social relations today with those of the past by describing informal prohibitions on social relations, similar to Jim Crow United States (Dollard 1937; Powdermaker 1939; Moody 1968). In his analysis of social relations between blacks and whites in Indianola, Mississippi, in the 1930s, John Dollard describes the foundations for this link: "[Among] the various Jim Crow customs which isolated colored people socially . . . the commonest of these taboos are those against eating at a table with Negroes, having them in the parlor of one's house as guests, sitting with them on the front porch of one's home, and the like. Any of these acts would imply social equality instead of social inferiority for the Negro" (1937, 351)

Blacks are not excluded from the homes (and kitchens) of Euro-Brazilians at present, as I learned from the *criado* stories that they told when asked to define racism.[1] Their definitions of racism was predicated on the *complete* exclusion of blacks from their homes. Thus, since blacks are included as members of their multiracial households (working as domestic servants), this is provided as evidence that there is no racism.

In Vasalia, criadas provide unpaid domestic service in middle-class and elite homes of their Euro-Brazilian adoptive families. They live and work under material and socioeconomic conditions similar to that of their slave ancestors. In her critique of Marxist feminist theories and theories of racial hierarchy, Evelyn Nakano Glenn (1992) has argued that both bodies of literature have failed to include an analysis of the racial division of reproductive labor. Glenn says: "The racial division of reproductive labor has been a missing piece of the picture in both literatures. This piece, I would contend, is key to the distinct exploitation women of color as a source of both hierarchy and interdependence among white women and women of color."

For the vast majority of Afro-Brazilian girls, whether light-skinned mulattas or dark-skinned pretas, their first work experience generally occurs in middle-class homes as the unpaid nursemaids, cooks, laundresses, and domestic servants of their white adoptive mothers. When asked to define racism, middle-class and elite Euro-Brazilians would point to their adoption of Afro-Brazilian children as an example of the *absence* of racism within their families. In her analysis of how reciprocity and dependency function, Nancy Scheper-Hughes (1992, 125) examines twenty-three wealthy and middle-class households. She quotes an elite white woman on her motivations for adopting a poor girl.

> I needed an extra maid. I asked Jose Costa . . . to find me a young
> girl from the rural area near Alianca. And so he drove to the villa
> during his lunch hour and he knocked on the door of a woman to
> whom he had been referred. . . . I have not made her into a slave the
> way some of the wealthy treat their foster children or the way our
> grandmothers and great grandmothers treated their adoptive
> children. . . . My own mother kept a black girl as a kind of slave, and
> when my mother died, I inherited her as a middle-aged woman, a
> childlike adult who had never married and didn't know anything other
> than taking care of my mother. . . . I kept her until she died.

This tradition of adoption is discussed by Stanley Stein. He links it to servitude and describes the benefits to the white elites. "After abolition, members of upper-class families often became the godparents of infants born to

FIGURE 6. Niara, an eleven-year-old criada, cares for the three white children under the age of six of her white adoptive mother. *(Photo by Jonathan Warren.)*

their former slaves. These were frequently raised in the godparent's homes in the expectation that they would become dedicated household servants" ([1958] 1985, 149).

Interviews with Afro-Brazilian and Euro-Brazilian women in Vasalia suggest that it is a common practice for Afro-Brazilian children to be adopted by middle- and upper-class Euro-Brazilian families to be raised as live-in servants until they marry or run away. When I hinted in private conversations that this might constitute exploitation, the Euro-Brazilians passionately defended the practice by arguing that they were "helping" these girls. Their narratives of "altruism" did not differ from those reported by Scheper-Hughes (1992). The practice of *criacão* (adoption) funnels Afro-Brazilian children, particularly girls, into a life of unpaid servitude. Using Afro-Brazilian children as laborors at a young age also assumes that black children are ideally suited for menial labor rather than education.

Carl Degler, a historian, offers this analysis of the statement of a white Brazilian businessman who was asked to comment on the treatment of Afro-Brazilians located in middle-class white households: "When reminded that some people, particularly the wealthy, seem to accept Negroes as members of their families, he compared the treatment of Negroes received with that 'the same persons dispensed to their house pets. They treat the Negroes as if they were a beloved puppy or kitten.' . . . 'It is clear,' he went on, 'that they do not treat the Negro as an equal. Also they would not think of confusing the Negro with a white'" (1971, 126).

Neither the Afro- nor Euro-Brazilians I interviewed mentioned the exploitation of the labor of Afro-Brazilian children when asked to define racism. Instead, both the Afro-Brazilians who had been raised by Euro-Brazilians and their adoptive parents claimed that their white families had "provided" for them. Euro-Brazilians described their relationships with these Afro-Brazilian domestic workers in sentimental and romantic terms, similar to those of U.S. whites who grew up being serviced by blacks in the Jim Crow South. They told stories of their *irmas* (sisters), who were not paid wages for helping around the house. Upper-middle-class whites whose families are currently raising Afro-Brazilian girls do not typically send these girls to primary school. They are trained only for domestic service. While their black "children" are required to work in the home, without receiving wages, their white children are sent to school and are not expected to engage in domestic chores.

Niara, an eleven-year-old dark-skinned Afro-Brazilian girl who lived a few houses away from me, was being exploited as a servant. An adopted child who was barely four feet tall, she was responsible for taking care of three children between two and five years old. She does not attend school regularly because of the demanding job of caring for these three grandchildren of her white adoptive mother.

In her definition of racism, Vera, a thirty-eight-year-old Italo-Brazilian schoolteacher, pointed to her grandparents' adoption of a black woman as evidence that her family was not racist. "My grandparents took in this black girl when she was very small to take care of my mother and all of their children in the house. . . . She was raised in our house and died within the family. What I am trying to say is that she never married. She remained the 'aunt' of all of the family, understand. I used to call her *tia*. I considered her a family member. She was there to take care of my mother. She was the *baba* (nurse-maid/child care worker) of my mother and all of her brothers."

Like the Aunt Jemima and Uncle Ben of the American South, Vera's description of her tia would be familiar to European-Americans who grew up in the pre–Civil War and pre–civil rights South. Vera's aunt is the asexual black mammy whose life centered around the needs of her white family. The memory of this tia is invoked by Vera to explain why she believed that her Italian grandparents were not racists. Their willingness to adopt a black girl whom they raised to be a lifelong servant was presented as evidence that they liked blacks.

Tia can be used as a term of endearment. For the purposes of my analysis of definitions of racism, I would like to examine its use as a power-evasive term, which transforms racial hierarchies of domestic labor into unremarkable multiracial households in which Afro-Brazilian children help the family. Using the word *tia* enables Vera to shift attention away from this Afro-Brazilian woman's status as an unpaid domestic servant and transforms her into a member of the family. Abdias do Nascimento describes this type of language: "Another trademark of the ideology of race mixture is the evocation of sentimental images of interracial affections, nurtured by such immortal stereotypes as the Black mammy/Aunt Jemima figure" (1989 [1979], 64).

Isabela, a thirty-four-year-old white self-employed business owner, described the daughter of her parents' *empregada* (domestic servant) in similar terms. Although married, Isabela and her husband have been living with her parents while saving money to buy the materials and land to construct a new home. She described her parents' servant as a family member and explained that "like other family members she doesn't receive wages for her services." Isabela stressed that this woman was treated in the *same* manner as other family members. She does not emphasize that this woman does not receive wages for the work she performs. On the other hand, Isabela pays her own husband, a *white* family member, a salary. Thus, some family members are paid wages for working for the family business. The justification for not paying the Afro-Brazilian woman a wage because she is a family member is contradicted by Isabela's payment of wages to her white family members. The daughter of her parents' maid is being raised in the same household.

> She also provides domestic services and runs errands for family members. Like her mother, she is learning to provide domestic services without expecting to receive a wage for any of the services she performs. . . . We took her in when she was twelve years old. She lives in our house . . . then she got her own bedroom, everything of her own. She *helps* my mother in the kitchen. But she doesn't cook. She is a negra. All of her relatives are also negras. She is treated normally like a [white] person. She is treated the same way we are so much so that she does not receive a salary. My father doesn't pay her a fixed wage. [My father] gives her money if she needs it. If she is in need, she asks my father. And my father will give her some money. She has an [illegitimate] daughter also. She is a single mother and has a black daughter who is also being raised in our home. She is one year older than my son. He is six years old today. She is being raised like our child also. If we are going on vacation, we bring her with us. Clothes, toys, all are equal. At Christmas, all the gifts [the children receive] are equal. Birthday parties, we do the same thing for her [the servant's daughter] that we do for my own son. We make a cake, everything. She is treated the *same* way, but this maid, she is more racist than any white person.

Note that Isabela attempts to minimize the power differences between her white son and the black daughter of her domestic servant by emphasizing the similar treatment that the two children separated by gender, race, and class receive in her home. She also minimizes any awareness that either child may have about their differential status on the basis of their gender, race, and class position within the household.

Ruth Frankenberg has described these discursive moves as "power evasive" in her research on U.S. white women. Kinship terms are used to avoid naming these women as servants: "A number of euphemisms used by these women appeared to serve the function of avoiding naming power. . . . There were also at times hints at the possibility that, for some women, descriptions of people of color that evaded naming race (and therefore power) formed what one might describe as a 'polite' or 'public' language of race that contrasted with other, private languages" (1993, 149). Thus Isabela can mask the power differential between her white (biological) son, with access to wealth as the son of two wage earners, and her maid's daughter, whose mother must request funds when they are needed, with evidence of their intimacy. The domestic servant is described as a family member, while in reality she is a worker who is given room and board and rarely cash.

In her analysis of women's political organizing during the 1970s and 1980s in Brazil, political theorist Sonia Alvarez reminds us that

> given the rigidity of class structure and racial hierarchies and the severity of income disparities and power imbalances in Brazil, we must also pay specific attention to the way in which class and race are constitutive of gender interests. . . . Moreover, one woman's strategic gender interests might threaten another's practical gender interests. A Latin American white middle-class, university-educated woman's practical gender interests, for example, might include the continuation of domestic service as an occupational category and could therefore come into direct conflict with the strategic gender interests of a dark-skinned working-class, illiterate woman who is her would-be domestic servant.(1990, 26)

Interestingly, I found *no* contrast between these sentimental portraits of middle-class and elite Euro-Brazilians and those of the poor Afro-Brazilians who had been raised as the adoptees of white families. I conducted extensive life history interviews with two women whose experience I was told by other residents was typical for dark skinned Afro-Brazilian women from poor families. I was introduced to Eliani, an unmarried, twenty-eight-year-old mother of a four-year-old son (who had been fathered by a white man whose name she did not reveal). Eliani had not completed five years of primary school. Her story was repeated as I encountered more and more women under the age of thirty who had worked their entire lives without receiving any wages, had not attained literacy, and had children fathered by white or lighter-skinned men. All told the same story of their "adoption" by a middle-class white woman.

Born in the city of Rio in 1964 to a poor Afro-Brazilian woman, Eliani was adopted by a white woman when she was two months old. She does not know the exact date of her birth since she was told by her white adoptive mother that her birth was never registered. Eliana had no information about her biological parents and no contact with any of her relatives. She has worked (without receiving wages) as a domestic servant in her white mother's home for eighteen years. She came to Vasalia several months ago in search of employment and was recently hired by Moema, an unmarried white teacher, to work for approximately $35.00 per month five days per week. Eliana describes this job as ideal because, since Moema has no children, Eliana is only required to cook for Moema and her mother and is off on Saturdays and Sundays. She can return home at night to perform chores for her adoptive mother.

When asked to define racism, Eliana told me that she had nothing to say. She has never heard the term *racismo* and has no idea what it means. She tells me that although there are "some whites who don't like blacks," she has never experienced racism. She had never discussed the issue and had never heard anyone else mention it.

This same position is further illustrated by Mani, a twenty-nine-year-old married woman with one child. When I first met Mani she was attending primary school at night and was functionally illiterate. When asked to describe her family of criacão, a wealthy white family, Mani's narrative did not differ from that of Isabela and of upper-middle-class Euro-Brazilians. She described how well she was treated by her white adoptive family. Mani appeared to be very grateful to have been raised in a white middle-class household although now she had no education and no material rewards to show for this. Without literacy skills, Mani now works part time cleaning a small grocery store.

During numerous informal conversations and a private interview, Mani had difficulty responding to any questions about racism. Although she described many situations that appeared to involve racial discrimination, she

FIGURE 7. Mani, a criada, and her husband and son. *(Photo by the author.)*

did not cite them when asked to provide examples of racism. Mani was reluctant to acknowledge that she had received any differential treatment (based on her dark skin color, African ancestry, and adoptive status) within her white family. She expressed no anger toward her white adoptive family for not providing her with the same level of education as their white children or for preventing her from completing primary school.

At the age of eleven, Mani was required to clean and cook full time while her white sisters continued attending school in preparation for the university entrance exam. This smooth transition from being a child who attends school to an unpaid domestic servant working full time is characteristic within white middle- and upper-middle-class households in Vasalia. Mani explains why she stopped attending primary school: "So I had to stop going to school in order to work in the house [as a maid]. . . . Yes. That's right. Up to a certain age, we [my white sister and I] were raised as equals. After I arrived at a certain age [eleven years old], I had to stop studying. That is why I recently started the fifth level of primary school now [at age thirty-one]. If it wasn't for cooking and cleaning the house all day, I would have graduated a long time ago."

When Mani was asked if she had chosen to stop attending primary school at age eleven, she replied: "No. I left because I was obliged to leave, understand? I had to work. I used to have to cook [for my adoptive family]. And this didn't leave me the time to go to school and to do the same things [as my white sister]. And during that time I stopped attending school because there was no night school. I was only eleven years old. I was too young to go to night school."

Mani was told that she could not continue her primary education because she could not be properly registered at school. The Brazilian public schools require a birth certificate in order to register children. Since Mani had been abandoned at the hospital by her mother shortly after birth, the registration papers had never been completed so her exact date of birth were unknown.

Mario, a fourth-generation Luso-Brazilian plantation owner, described the treatment of his black adoptive sister in a way that suggests it is unusual for these girls to secure more than primary school education: "I still have an adoptive sister, a black girl. She graduated [from secondary school] while she lived in the home of my parents. There were two blacks raised with me.

FIGURE 8. The country residence of a white elite family. *(Photo by the author.)*

She studied until she became a teacher. Today she teaches. She did this and in my house she was treated like our sister." His sister's ability to obtain an education while living in "my" house was mentioned by Mario with pride, which suggests that this is not a common occurrence. Like all the wealthy and middle-class Euro-Brazilians I interviewed, Mario uses familial terms such as *sister* to emphasize the *shared* status while minimizing any power and status differentials that existed in his home.

These criado stories are important because they illuminate the paradigms that Vasalians use when they define racism. By defining racism as the absolute social exclusion of blacks from Euro-Brazilian households, the exploitation of Afro-Brazilian children and adults as unpaid domestic servants can be framed as multiracial families in which the darker-skinned children "help" with domestic chores.

The Village Club and Dances

George Reid Andrews identifies middle-class social clubs as one of the remaining obstacles to Afro-Brazilian upward mobility in São Paulo: "For the Brazilian middle and upper classes, the social clubs are one of the most important mechanisms of social integration and advancement available to them: and for those unable to gain admission, the clubs function as one of the most effective means of social and economic exclusion. As a result, the clubs have constituted one of the most difficult hurdles for Afro-Brazilians to get over" (1991, 173).

When I spoke with Afro-Brazilian professionals, all described white opposition to their participation in middle-class social events and in the Village Social Club as a common form of racism that they experienced. They offered examples of both formal and informal practices that had the explicit intention of prohibiting Afro-Brazilian participation in social events. Maria, a forty-year-old Brazilian of African descent, who describes herself as a morena, speaks of racism during her youth.

> There was a Club of Thirteen that they held on Fridays . . . where the Secretary of Education is now located today. In the past it was called the Club of Thirteen. Only those that were wealthy and white went there. Then they used to have a dance every season. A special dance was held for the spring when they invited the wealthy. . . . They used to make new clothes. No one was able to copy the clothing and hair designs of another person. It was all kept secret, hair, nails, these things. Only whites were allowed to attend these events. . . . If a black came to the door, he was prohibited from entering.

In Vasalia, the exclusion of Afro-Brazilians, particularly dark-skinned negros, was considered a typical example of racism. Social clubs assume a critical role in the integration of Afro-Brazilians into middle-class life. Every dark-skinned Afro-Brazilian interviewed reported that they faced opposition from the Euro-Brazilian club administrators. This opposition was not based on their socioeconomic status, but on skin color and race.

Carlucci's mother, Tatiana, is a fifty-two-year-old housewife. She is married to a city employee, whom she describes as a negro. Her family is the sole family of Afro-Brazilians residing on the most prestigious of the three main streets with a self-identified black head of household. She gave an example of how middle-class Afro-Brazilians were rejected solely on the basis of their color when they applied for membership at the Village Social Club.

> I used to go to [the Village Country Club] but I was not treated well by [the white members] and I am not welcomed by them. When the

FIGURE 9. A typical two-story business and residence of a white middle-class family on the main street. *(Photo by the author.)*

[Village Club] was inaugurated, the people of our color [mulattos] wanted to buy a membership. We had enough money to purchase a membership but [the white administrator] wouldn't sell us a membership because of our skin color. Only in the end, after they sold membership titles to all of the whites, then they would sell to an exceptional black. It depended upon your job and such things. But they didn't want to sell to people of color. There were people with the money in their hands. They told them that they had sold out of all the memberships and that they could not sell any more . . . but that same day one of the blacks whom they had denied a membership loaned the same money to a white girl. She went there to the club and they sold her a membership that same day.

Those dark-skinned Afro-Brazilians who were not denied membership often faced subtle forms of social exclusion and withdrew *voluntarily* from the club. The Afro-Brazilian professionals interviewed recognized but did not directly challenge the covert forms of racism that denied them from full participation in the club.

> My father bought a membership in this club for us. For me, I went to the club only once because I automatically felt bad. . . . It wasn't that I didn't know most of the people in the club. In a small city, everyone knows each other . . . but I think people spoke like this, "Ah, now we're going to go there [in the swimming pool] and get *moreninha* (get dirtied/darkened)." In their minds, they were saying "What is that black going to do here, burn or what?" So I automatically didn't feel comfortable . . . they [white members] could never imagine that I [a black person] was going to refresh myself the same way they would, to go with the same intention. Or that I was there to shoot the breeze [socialize] and drink a beer like a normal person. The first thing they did was stare at me.

Another social milieu that Afro-Brazilian men described when asked for examples of racism are public dances held either at the Village Club or in other public spaces. Afro-Brazilian men often spoke of their rejection by white women as dance partners at social events that do not exclude Afro-Brazilians from attending. Carlucci describes an incident in which he was rejected as a desirable partner by his Euro-Brazilian female peers.

> During adolescence you begin to discover the world. You begin to get to know girls. I used to go to parties in order to socialize with the girls. I planned social events in order to accomplish this. The white girls only sought out the whites and I was one of the few blacks who participated in this social group. I was always left behind, always excluded. They dated among each other but no one would ever select me as a dance partner. So I suffered a little with this problem in my adolescence. This suffering included having young white women who were drunk out of their minds say "I'm so drunk that I am even willing to [become the lover of] Carlucci tonight." This made me feel rejected.

When asked whether he had ever encountered racism, Eduardo, a twenty-one-year-old Afro-Brazilian, described a pattern of behavior by the

Euro-Brazilian women he pursued. White women, when they encountered disapproval for their interracial socialization with him, promptly discontinued the relationship. "I have been rejected at wedding receptions. I noticed this at a particular party that I attended. For example, I am a brown man and I was accompanied by a *loira* (blond woman). She was interested in dating me but because of what other people said she decided not to date me and won't even speak to me in public. It is much easier for me to date a brown or black woman than a white woman."

No Afro-Brazilian interviewed cited the rejection of dark-skinned Afro-Brazilians by lighter-skinned Afro-Brazilians as desirable dating or marital partners when asked to define racism. This demonstrates the extent to which Euro-Brazilians serve as the social reference group for Afro-Brazilians.[2]

The Sexual Sphere

Another variation on the theme of social segregation is opposition to interracial sexual relationships and interracial marriage. In providing specific examples of racism, Afro-Brazilians typically described situations of support or opposition to their romantic relationships with whites. In a similar vein, Euro-Brazilians would point to their families' acceptance or prohibition of interracial marriage.

"I'm not a racist. I really love mulattas," is how Euro-Brazilian men would initially respond to questions that I posed about their commonsense understandings of racism. As a woman who was defined in local terms as a mulatta, I would be repeatedly told by white men that they adored mulattas. Their *sexual* desire for mulattas was repeatedly mentioned as evidence of their racial egalitarianism. The erotic sphere of interracial romance is the arena that typically emerged in casual discussions with Afro-Brazilian women and Euro-Brazilian men of working-class backgrounds in their analysis of racial egalitarianism and inequality.

When asked for examples of racism, the Afro-Brazilians interviewed, like their Euro-Brazilian counterparts, thought of interracial sexual and romantic relationships, but Afro-Brazilians did not consider their reluctance or refusal to date or marry other Afro-Brazilians (particularly dark-skinned persons) as racist. An illustration of the typical response of Afro-Brazilian women has been taken from a taped interview with Catarina, an unmarried, dark-skinned, twenty-seven-year-old Afro-Brazilian primary school teacher. In answer to the question "Does racism exist in Vasalia?" Catarina replies, "No. Dating between the races is not prohibited here. I have a white boyfriend." Thus, she denies the existence of racism on the basis of her access to a white boyfriend. State-sanctioned forms of sociosexual segregation by race as encoded in law are her point of reference.

Carlucci, the son of Tatiana, is a tall, charismatic, and dignified twenty-three-year-old self-described *negro*, who works as a clerk in the mayor's office. He completed secondary school but could not afford to pay for the *vestibular*, the one-year course in which middle- and upper-class Euro-Brazilians enroll to prepare for the university entrance exams. He described the rejection and disapproval he has experienced when he has attempted to socialize with white female peers:

> There is a *senhor* here called [name]. I used to be very good friends
> with his daughter. And I was always invited to their house, under-
> stand. Her father was the type of guy who drank quite a bit, a drunk.
> I am trying to say that he didn't have any shame, wasn't afraid to
> say what he was thinking. He used to say these [racist] things and I
> sensed that he didn't approve of my presence in his home. . . . My
> friend [his daughter] used to invite me to have lunch with them and
> [her father] would always start joking . . . "What is going on here?
> Blacks have to eat outside in the yard. Send this nigger outside." . . . I
> was offended by this statement and I believe that if I had attempted
> to date his daughter, he would have opposed our relationship.

Even when Afro-Brazilian men managed to establish a stable romantic relationship with a Euro-Brazilian, they reported being routinely humiliated. Their relationships were not affirmed by the Euro-Brazilian community. Carlucci is currently dating Monisha, a nineteen-year-old woman of African and European descent, who is described as a *morena clara* (in this case, a light-skinned brunette) by middle-class Euro-Brazilians and a branca by working-class Afro- and Euro-Brazilians. When he describes the public response to his relationships with former white girlfriends and Monisha, similar levels of overt disapproval of emerge. "When I used to walk down the street with [white girlfriends] in the case of the loira and with Monisha, I feel the stares of people, understand. Nothing precise is ever said but I felt that [the community] did not support our romance. Including comments as we walked

FIGURE 10. Carlucci, Tatiana's son, and his fiancée, Monisha. *(Photo by the author.)*

by such as 'This type of man with a pretty branca. How could you choose a black [for a lover]?'"

The quotation reveals the public pressure placed on Euro-Brazilian women who do not reject dark-skinned Afro-Brazilian men as lovers. Monisha's logic is questioned by the public. Why would she, as an attractive white-skinned woman, select a black man as her lover when she could acquire a more desirable lover?

Other informants, particularly working-class Euro-Brazilians, emphasized their acceptance of dark-skinned Afro-Brazilians in their extended family as evidence that racism did not exist in Vasalia. Responding to the same question "Does racism exist in Vasalia?" Vittorio, a fifty-four-year-old retired military soldier, poet, and the grandson of Italian immigrants, immediately said how much the male members of his family adored mulattas. He proceeded to name all of his Afro-Brazilian relatives by marriage. His nephew, a third-generation Italian-Brazilian of very poor origins, married a light-skinned Afro-Brazilian. This marriage was presented as evidence that racism did not exist in his family and that it was not common among Italian-Brazilians. Vittorio argued, "I don't know if you heard this but a person

FIGURE 11. Vittorio, a published poet and retired military officer, with his family. *(Photo by Jonathan Warren.)*

of Italian origin, people that have the blood of Italy, 99 percent of them like mulattos. The majority of them like mulattos." What Vittorio did not mention is that when his nephew, Allesandro, married a mulatta, his brother (Vittorio's other nephew) and Allesandro's grandmother (Vittorio's mother) refused to ever visit because of their strong disapproval of the marriage.

In stark contrast to Vittorio's portrayal of Italians as being free of racism, Mario, a fifty-two-year-old Luso-Brazilian plantation owner, argued that if there was any racism in Vasalia, the Italians, not the Portuguese, are to blame because the Italians oppose marriage with blacks. "I think racism exists today because of the Italians who immigrated here. They don't like blacks. They used to think that blacks couldn't marry an Italian because normally Italians are white . . . the old ones. I used to hear them say that they were opposed to race mixture."

Euro-Brazilian men interviewed simultaneously acknowledge that white opposition to interracial marriage exits, while also maintaining their innocence by shifting the responsibility to the other Euro-Brazilian group. This strategy enables Euro-Brazilians to frame racism as a problem for which they are not responsible because it is someone else's fault.

Allesandro, Vittorio's thirty-three-year-old nephew, provides a more dramatic example of white opposition to an interracial marriage, which resulted in the assassination of a poor Afro-Brazilian man by hired gunmen.

> The incident that I am going to tell you is about a [white] *fazendeiro* (plantation owner). It happened here—in this region. His [white] daughter wanted to marry a poor young man working in the rural zone. And he didn't want his daughter to marry this type [black]. . . . He found and ordered many men to kill this poor young man. And what really happened is that they murdered him. . . . And so the wedding didn't occur . . . she just married a [white] man who is also poor but this is because she was already pregnant by this man whom they killed.

If we compare the responses of poor and working-class Euro-Brazilians to those of the middle- and upper-middle classes in this community, we find the same emphasis on interracial romantic and marital relationships. However, elite Euro-Brazilians point to their families' opposition, not acceptance, of light- and dark-skinned Afro-Brazilians. No one interviewed could point to a single case of interracial marriage involving a local Euro-Brazilian upper-class woman or man and an Afro-Brazilian.

In her discussion of racism, Isabela, a thirty-four-year-old self-employed business owner, argues that her family would have opposed her marriage to an Afro-Brazilian man. Her characterization of Afro-Brazilians as undesirable marriage partners was typical among the middle- and upper-class Euro-Brazilians interviewed. "If I had dated a mulatto or black man, I think that my father . . . I know that my father, he or someone in my family would have interfered. He would have said 'Oh my God! But he is black, or he is a mulatto.' We say that we are not racists, but . . . in reality if we were to have a romantic life with a black man, relationships with my family members would change."

The elites interviewed made *no* distinction between mulattos and negros, that is, between lighter- and darker-skinned Afro-Brazilians. Both groups are equally undesirable as marital partners.

A successful forty-one-year-old white man, Doctor Giovanni, who married one of the great-granddaughters of the Italian-Portuese elite families, provides his definition of racism. Like Isabela, he defines racism as his family's opposition to interracial marriage. He says that he was taught that Afro-Brazilians are not acceptable marital partners.

> As always, [racism] was disguised. Racism is not something that is explicitly defined. It was never said that "we are going to discuss racial inequality" but in family gatherings, during lunch . . . racial inequality was approached in the following manner. For me, this was always said very explicitly. My grandmother was of European origin, very light-skinned, and very blue eyes, a Portuguese woman. Back then, she used to always say, "If God had wanted people to be [treated] equally, he would have made them look the same. Therefore if he cast them in different colors, one white and the other black, it is because he wanted them to be treated differently." Thus, this was the perspective of my grandmother. In my family, they would say, as everyone in Brazil says, there is no racism here. Everyone is equal. I observed this very clearly: blacks served us [as maids]. Blacks came to our home. Blacks ate with us, as friends. However, if you were to date a black or if anyone in the family loved a black person, the situation would change. "Ah, no!" my mother, for example, used to say. "Ah, How could I look at my black grandchildren. My mulatto grandchildren with their kinky hair!" Then it became clear. I am trying to say that for friendship, for studying together, for socializing, to bring blacks into our home to serve us and prepare our meals, this is fine. But to enter our family, to become part of our family. No!

This clearly shows how the boundaries of interracial social interaction are established within upper-middle-class Euro-Brazilian families. Once again, there is inclusion of blacks in white families as casual friends or servants, giving the appearance of racial equality. The testimony also illustrates how polite interracial relationships are sustained even while transmitting beliefs in racial separatism and black racial inferiority to white children.

Invisible Forms of Racism

I have described the parameters of definitions of racism in Vasalia. What forms of racism cannot be accounted for by the local definitions that I have delineated? Social scientists have documented several types that remain outside the parameters of local concepts of racism.

In the following section, I discuss several of these forms and provide a typology of them. They are significant because they have been used as evidence of racial inequality (particularly by quantitative sociologists and antiracist activists). In Vasalia, there is a disjuncture between the measures of racism used by local residents and by scholars. For example, in my interviews with the Afro-Brazilians, they all failed to consider socioeconomic, semiotic, and institutional forms of racism.[3] To my surprise, the Vasalians who did explicitly identify the aesthetic arena and institutions as places where racism operated were Euro-Brazilians.

The Semiotic Contours of Racism: Representations of Afro-Brazilians

It was the last week of summer vacation. Carla and Catarina, two Afro-Brazilian primary school teachers, were in a heightened state of excitement as they prepared for the first week of classes. They both taught at the same Catholic primary school. After we watched *Peruas Perigosas*, their favorite telenovela, they asked me to help them prepare personalized assignment books for their students. That evening we sat down with construction paper, drawing pencils, and markers. From my position as a brown-skinned, brown-eyed, brown-haired, U.S. black, I watched in astonishment as Carla and Catarina, brown-skinned and brown-eyed women, repeatedly drew images of exclusively blond, blue-eyed children to illustrate all of their grading books. This continued into the night as they produced exclusively white images for their classroom wall posters.

Several weeks later, Carla and Catarina invited me to their school to talk about race relations in the United States. When I went to visit their school I commented on the absence of any visual images of brown-eyed, brown-skinned, or brunette Brazilians in the school classrooms. When I attempted to engage the teachers in a discussion about their production of images that I considered both racist and not reflective of the actual appearance of the majority of students, they accused me of being an antiwhite racist. It became evident that I had more expansive definitions of what constitutes racism than they did.

The definitions of racism that I employed considered access to the media and the distribution of power along economic and political lines. For me, the "repetitive absences" of Afro-Brazilians and dark-skinned people, except as "traditional Africans," in Brazilian school textbooks and in the classroom were a form of racism. However, for Catarina and Carla these images were unremarkable. I agree with researchers of Brazilian racial inequality who have argued that textual and visual images are not innocent (Simpson 1993; Hanchard 1994). Thus, in contrast to the teachers interviewed, I considered the visual content of the classroom visual materials a central site for the transmission of racist ideologies. As political scientist Michael Hanchard notes:

> From the first years of formal education, blacks are confronted by a panoply of images and representations of themselves, which can only be characterized as negative. Numerous studies of children's primary textbooks depict blacks as more sexually promiscuous and aggressive, intellectually inferior to whites, and rarely in positions of power. Specifically black males are often represented as brawny types, long on stamina and physical strength and short on intellect. Black women are portrayed as a form of "superwoman," an image found in evocations of women of African descent throughout the Western literature. (1994, 60)

Several studies of school textbooks and institutional racism in the public school system conducted in the mid-1980s found that when blacks are presented in school textbooks they are depicted in a grotesque style and caricatured as animals. Furthermore, black characters are less often given names (Pinto 1987; Silva 1987; Rosemberg 1990). In an analysis of racism in the public schools in the city of Rio de Janeiro, Vera Moreira Figueira (1990) concluded that in school textbooks blacks are: (1) depicted as the social inferiors of whites, (2) not portrayed in families, (3) stereotyped as similar to animals, (4) excluded from references in history or social science texts, and (5) when mentioned in history textbooks, Afro-Brazilian contributions were limited to traditional Africans.[4] Although researchers might agree that these images of blacks are racist, this study does not tell us whether the Afro-Brazilian students attending these schools perceived these images as racist.

The representations analyzed by Figueira that depict Afro-Brazilians in derogatory ways are not considered racist by the Afro-Brazilians I knew in Vasalia. These images, which I saw on the kitchen walls of white elite homes and in the textbooks of Vasalian students, were never commented on in discussions of racism.

In *Xuxa: The Mega-Marketing of Gender, Race, and Modernity*, Amelia Simpson (1993) argues that the blond, blue-eyed Brazilian television star Xuxa exemplifies an aesthetic hierarchy that privileges and valorizes whiteness.[5] This valorization of whiteness is naturalized in Brazil. Not one Vasalian whom I interviewed identified the Xuxa show or other television shows that depict Afro-Brazilian primarily as laughing buffoons, mammies, dancing mulattas, and prostitutes as racist. Although there has been some recent introduction of middle-class Afro-Brazilian families to the television novellas, this arena was not identified as one where racial inequality operates.

When considering how to strategically intervene in media constructions of race that reproduce racist ideologies in Britain, Stuart Hall has argued: "For very complex reasons, a sort of racist 'common sense' has become pervasive in our society. And the media frequently work from this common sense, taking it as their base-line without questioning it. We need, urgently, to consider ways in which, *in addition* to the urgent and necessary political task of blocking the path to power of the openly organized racist and right extremist organizations, we can also begin to construct an antiracist common sense" (1981, 28).

Researchers have extensively documented the lack of access that Afro-Brazilians have to positive representations of themselves in the popular press, textbooks, television, and other media forms (Pinto 1987; Silva 1987; Figueira 1990; Hanchard 1994). In his book on the negro movimento in Brazil, Hanchard interviewed an Afro-Brazilian antiracist activist who points out the important role that U.S. blacks played by producing positive images of blackness for Afro-Brazilians.

"At the end of 1969 . . . I started seeing and buying black American magazines, *Ebony* principally, which in this period had a revolutionary rhetoric. This journal (*Ebony*) reflected what was occurring in the civil rights and nationalist movements in the world, and it reflected this in a very strong way, especially the aesthetics element, the Afro-hairstyle and Afro clothing. It was love at first sight. . . . It was a new images of blacks that came from the United States." The "new image" to which [the activist] referred was novel for black Brazilians in two important respects . . . what black Brazilians were witnessing, perhaps for the first time, were people they resembled constructing oppositional, positive images of themselves in contradistinction to the West.(Hanchard 1994, 95)

In a study of Brazilian television, Conrad Kottak learned that "another striking culturally derived contrast between American and Brazilian television is in the representation of *dark-skinned characters*. Although Brazil is sometimes called a racial democracy, blacks, who are just as obvious in the Brazilian as in the American population, are much rarer on Brazilian television" (1990, 51).

Vasalians do not consider the absence of positive representations of dark-skinned Afro-Brazilians and the denigration of features that signify African ancestry when they are asked to define racism. The comments of Carlucci, a twenty-two-year-old dark-skinned Afro-Brazilian, who describes himself as a negro, illustrate the impact of these representations on the self-esteem of Afro-Vasalians: "I feel a little bad, you know. It's all right that blue eyes are beautiful . . . and the straight hair too. . . . They think that we are inferior. Consequently we *are* uglier. . . . And to be inferior is to be uglier. So when I hear comments about how blacks are ugly and whites are beautiful or when I feel what they are thinking, I feel inferior." Afro-Brazilians in Vasalia find it difficult to generate an alternative aesthetic that does not devalue their own features.

Eduardo, a nephew of Henrique, made similar comments. Eduardo, a twenty-one-year-old dark-brown-skinned Afro-Brazilian military police officer, prefers lighter-skinned Euro-Brazilian women, although he is currently dating a light-skinned Afro-Brazilian woman. He argued that "it's very difficult to find a pretty dark-skinned person." His cousin, Jorge, a twenty-two-year-old who dates white women exclusively, offered this comment: "The majority of blacks don't have good physical features. It's always the whites who are the most beautiful. Don't you think I'm right?"

What I found most surprising is that none of the Afro-Brazilians interviewed considered aesthetic hierarchies when asked to define racism. In

FIGURE 12. Dona Conceição, a member of an elite wine-making family in Vasalia, and Selma Oliviera. Her family maintains a tradition brought from Italy and produces a wine for which Vasalia is famous. *(Photo by the author.)*

contrast, several Euro-Brazilians did recognize the overvaluation of white skin, straight hair, light eyes, and features associated with Europeans such as thin lips as an expression of racism.

The Educational and Socioeconomic Spheres

Dimensions of racial inequality that were *not* included in definitions of racism, particularly by Afro-Brazilians, are literacy and access to higher education. Sociologists who have conducted statistical analyses have documented extensive racial disparities between whites and nonwhites in their analyses of the following: (1) completion of primary school, (2) completion of secondary school, (3) ability to transform an education into a higher income, (4) literacy rates, and (5) access to a university education. Numerous studies have concluded that pardos and pretos are disadvantaged in relation to brancos. For example, Nelson do Valle Silva and Carlos Hasenbalg (1992) have noted the overrepresentation of brancos and the underrepresentation of

Afro-Brazilians (pardos and pretos) in higher education in Brazil. In Vasalia, there are three Afro-Brazilians among the sixty public school teachers. There were two Afro-Brazilians teaching in the private (Catholic) elementary schools. Four of the five Afro-Brazilians teaching in the public and private schools belonged to one family.

Among the Afro-Brazilian interviewed, none commented upon the exclusion of Afro-Brazilians from the universities when asked to define racism. The only person who considered higher education as an arena where racism operates was Paulo, a fifty-two-year-old working-class Euro-Brazilian who had grown up in Rio de Janeiro but moved to Vasalia ten years ago when he married a local Afro-Brazilian woman.

> For me racism is the following. You are white and do not want to lose your space in order to allow room for a person of a different color. For me this is racism, understand. Because you can observe this easily, go to the university. You will see forty or fifty whites [in a university classroom] and only two to three blacks. Why are there forty whites and only two to three blacks? Because blacks are degraded. Whites don't give blacks access to a college education, to having a good education in order to achieve the same level that whites achieve.

This type of critique was never offered by any of the Afro-Brazilians I interviewed. It never emerged in casual conversations. The Afro-Brazilians argue that since they are not *formally* prohibited by law from entering an institution, that racism is not the reason for their exclusion from universities and higher education. The absence of *state-sanctioned* barriers to access to education is emphasized; informal, de facto forms of exclusion are rarely considered. An example of this can be taken from an interview with Fernando, one of the two best-educated Afro-Brazilian male professionals whom I interviewed. He was also described as one of the two wealthiest Afro-Brazilian men in the community by Vasalians from a range of backgrounds.[6] "I never encountered racism. I was never a victim of this. No. . . . I have always had free access to all places. I have never been restricted because of my race. I was allowed to take the university entrance exam. I passed. I was placed in one of the openings. I studied. I never noticed any racism among my colleagues."

On his office wall, in the gas station that he owned and operated, hung a photograph of his law school class. Out of approximately four hundred students, I counted about four individuals who were of obvious African ancestry (all men). When I asked Fernando about the representation of blacks and *pessoas de cor* (people of color) among his classmates, he replied, "There were plenty. . . . In 1972 there were four hundred students. How many of the day students were black, I cannot calculate this but at night we had—maybe ten." Fernando's interpretation of ten nonwhite students as "plenty" reveals his low expectations regarding nonwhite enrollment and how the almost complete absence of blacks was not interpreted as a consequence of racial hierarchies and racial exclusion. As long as blacks were not legally denied the right to take the entrance exam, Fernando did not perceive any institutional racism.

Sociologists analyzing racial inequalities in Brazil have found a strong correlation between having white skin and completing secondary education. In their analysis of the educational trajectories of groups by color in Brazil, sociologists Nelson do Valle Silva and Carlos Hasenbalg (1992) found that whites, as a group, are more likely than nonwhites to complete eight years of primary school. "To have white skin in Brazil represents the privilege of having 8.5 times more chances in comparison to blacks and almost five times more probability relative to browns of access to a university [education]. In this aspect of distribution between groups of color the opportunities of entering higher education in Brazil approximate South Africa more than the U.S., where in 1980, whites had opportunities 1.4 times greater than blacks entering this educational level."[7]

The orthodox interpretation of this data is that *socioeconomic status* is the reason for the lower level of educational achievement of nonwhites. Class inequality is undoubtedly one factor that contributes to this. However, in Silva and Hasenbalg's analysis of income and education, they found that among whites and nonwhites with the same level of education, an income gap remained.

None of the nonteachers and teachers interviewed privately could identify any Afro-Brazilian from Vasalia who had completed university education.[8] Nor are Afro-Brazilians studying for the *vestibular*, the university entrance exam. Again, the disproportionate number of Euro-Brazilians who complete *segunda grau* (secondary school) and *fez faculdade* (complete university training) was not cited by Afro-Brazilians as a measure of racial inequality.

Institutional Racism

The absence of Afro-Brazilians among plantation owners, store owners, sales representatives, politicians, and judges was also never considered in definitions of racism. In the next chapter, I discuss in more detail the explanations people give to rationalize their absence. I want to call attention here to the fact that the concept of proportional representation of Afro-Brazilians in institutions was never invoked in Vasalian definitions of racism.

The absence of formal, written, and overtly declared antiblack policies is the criterion that Vasalians typically used when they thought of racism. They rarely thought of the absence of Afro-Brazilians from these industries. When these absences were considered, it was Euro-Brazilians, not Afro-Brazilians, who mentioned it. However, the Euro-Brazilians did not believe that this type of institutional racism operated in Vasalia.

The concept of *institutional racism* was theorized by black activists such as Stokely Carmichael and Charles Hamilton (1967). Their theories were further developed by and expanded upon by sociologists such as Robert Blauner (1972). This concept enabled U.S. blacks to shift the emphasis away from individual attitudes and intentions to institutional practices and structures that sustained white supremacy. Vasalians did not use this concept. They repeatedly described racism in terms of *individual* attitudes and practices.

Euro-Brazilians sometimes gave examples of what I considered to be institutional racism. But, while recognizing that racism occurred, they tended to frame it as unique instances. An example of the form of racism that is not typically recognized is illustrated by the comments of Paulo, a fifty-four-year-old working-class white man who moved to Vasalia ten years ago when he married a local woman. Paulo responds to the question "Can you provide any examples of racism?"

> This happened in the firms that I worked for in Rio, in aeronautics. Also in the navy [racial discrimination occurred]. They did not accept people of color. How did I know this? I used to see [racism]. They didn't openly say this, "No! Blacks are not able to enlist or work in this organization. We don't want blacks in the aviation

industry." No, they didn't say this. But I sensed that [whites] didn't want them working there. And when I used to do the enrollment, or when I made a list or anything, they didn't approve of the people of color who applied [for positions]. They didn't allow them to work there. So only whites, blonds entered the industry. Blonds were preferred. People that had blond hair, understand. In many situations, Brazilian firms . . . also Sears, which is American, the same thing occurred, [whites] didn't accept blacks in their administration.

Although now balding, Paulo had been blond-haired and was in an ideal position to witness these unstated practices. These are the types of informal practices that generate de facto, all-white employment but that don't require explicit rejection of Afro-Brazilians. However, since only official policies are considered, this form of institutional racism remains outside the predominant definitions used in Vasalia.

The Racial Distribution of Political Power: Elected Officials

Electoral politics is another arena where racism operates in Brazil. This has been identified by scholars as a primary obstacle to black mobilization in Brazil. George Reid Andrews notes the lack of support from black voters for black candidates who openly address racism in their campaign. "Brazilian racial ideology offers them such strong incentives to ignore a problem which rarely takes overt, physical form, that relatively few of them [black voters] respond to black activists' call for a movement to combat racism. As a result, in both 1982 and 1986, middle-class black candidates throughout Brazil went down to defeat" (1991, 199).

In Vasalia, as in other regions of Brazil, Afro-Brazilians are underrepresented in positions in elected government.[9] In November 1992, Vasalians elected their first mayor, a wealthy Euro-Brazilian man with blond hair and blue eyes. They also elected a council board consisting of nine white men from the plantation-owning aristocracy. Although several Afro-Brazilian men ran for public office, neither won a seat on the city council. In casual conversation and in formal interviews, no one ever voluntarily commented upon the *whiteness* of the city council or the complete absence of Afro-Brazilians from elected positions as evidence of racial inequality.

When asked to define racism, none of the Vasalians considered the virtual absence of Afro-Brazilians from elected positions in the federal, state, and local government. I was repeatedly reminded by both Afro- and Euro-Brazilians that Afro-Brazilians are not legally prevented from running for public office, thus, if they weren't elected, it was not a consequence of racism.

Conclusion

In this chapter I have explored how racism is defined and commonly conceptualized in Vasalia. My analysis of Vasalian definitions of racism shifts the analysis away from U.S.-based definitions of racism, and from the criteria typically employed by U.S.-trained researchers, to the ideological terrain of ordinary Brazilians. By asking how Brazilians define racism, I identify one terrain of common usage that will have to be transformed if antiracist activists are to be successful in generating grassroots support for antiracist organizing.

I have argued that Vasalians use restricted criteria when asked to define racism. When theorizing about what constitutes an act of racism, the Brazilians interviewed typically considered only practices of exclusion in the social and sexual spheres, while not considering racial disparities in the socioeconomic, semiotic, educational, and political spheres.

These definitions of racism have implications for theorists and antiracist activists. Given these restricted definitions of racism that emphasize the social and sexual spheres, several forms of racism that have been documented by scholars of Brazilian racial inequality are not recognized in this community. Thus, indifference to racial inequality and antiracist organizing can be attributed, at least in part, to narrowly defined conceptualizations of racism. This suggests that the quantitative analyses of racial disparities may not be accepted by Vasalians as reliable measures of racism because these measures assume institutional racism, a form of racism not typically recognized in this community. Finally, definitions of racism that restrict racism to interactions in the sociosexual sphere promote racial harmony by not recognizing complex and covert forms of institutional racism.

CHAPTER 4

Discourses in Defense of the Racial Democracy

[Antonio Gramsci] . . . helps us to understand one of the most common, least explained features of "racism": the "subjection" of victims of racism to the mystifications of the very racist ideologies which imprison and define them.
—Stuart Hall (1986, 27)

The prevalence of the ideology of racial democracy among Blacks and whites was confusing for the foreign researcher. . . . The foreign researcher would point to example after example of seemingly blatant discrimination or attitudes indicative of racial prejudice only to be told by Afro-Brazilians that one had not understood the reality or social context of the situation, or all of the mitigating factors and circumstances.
—J. Michael Turner (1985, 76)

What remains from the previous belief system of racial democracy and earlier notions of racial exceptionalism is the denial of the existence of the ongoing racial oppression of Afro-Brazilians.
—Michael Hanchard (1994, 56)

*I*n the previous chapter I mapped the ideological terrain of commonsense understandings of racism. I argued that a disjuncture exists between criteria used by researchers to measure racial inequalities and criteria used by Afro- and Euro-Brazilians in Vasalia. In this chapter I analyze the discourses Vasalians use to account for the racial disparities in their community. How do they interpret what I, as a U.S. black researcher, perceive as patterns of racialized inequalities? In a context in which whites have a virtual monopoly on power, how do they discursively defend their faith in the *democracia racial*? Answers to these questions emerged in the responses to my inquiries about the whiteness of the local elite.

In their analysis of the racist discourse of New Zealanders, Wetherell and Potter explain their approach to discourse analysis:

> The context in which our study is situated is thus quite different from post-structuralism. Where that tradition has been analytic . . . it has focused overwhelmingly on images and texts, often from literature and philosophy. What post-structuralism has not done is address everyday discourse—people's talk and argument—nor has it been concerned with materials which document interaction of one kind or another. In some ways then our general aim is to pursue a post-structuralist question . . . but in a domain of materials which have been most thoroughly explored by ethnomethodologists and conversation analysts. (1992, 89)

Like Wetherall and Potter, I am motivated by a concern with "everyday talk and argument" in Vasalia. I am interested in the interpretive repertoires Vasalians employ to defend their belief in the Brazilian racial democracy in a context of pervasive racism. My aim is to map those discourses that Vasalians offer as an alternative to my suggestion that racial inequality is a fundamental feature of their life. The discourses that I analyze were presented as explanations for the absence of Afro-Brazilians as politicians, church officials, business owners, landowners, professionals, and other positions of prestige and power.

The Invisibility of White Privilege

In daily conversations there is no need to explain the whiteness of the local elite. The absence of Afro-Brazilians from the ranks of the elite is unremarkable. As an outsider, I would ask Vasalians to explain what they took for granted—the supremacy of whites. In *Outline of a Theory of Practice*, French sociologist Pierre Bourdieu (1977) provides a conceptual model that can be used to examine the invisibility of white privilege in Vasalia.

Bourdieu defines *doxa* as the "commonsense assumptions about the world through which individuals interpret and make sense out of events." As the "commonsense world," doxa is invisible precisely because it is assumed (1977, 159). The predominance of Euro-Brazilians among the economic, political, religious, and social elite in Vasalia is taken for granted and thus not visible. Thus, during my period of fieldwork, I never heard the whiteness of the elite commented on in public.

Not one Vasalian interviewed was able to identify a single wealthy Afro-Brazilian of *local* origins. No one could provide the name of a single Afro-Brazilian landowner, plantation owner, priest, or elected official. The exclusion of Afro-Brazilians from virtually every job category except as agricultural laborers, athletes, manual laborers, truck drivers, domestic servants, and the occasional primary school teacher appeared to require no explanation in everyday conversation. Although there were occasional *moments* when the whiteness of the elite became visible, no sustained critiques of racial inequality emerged in private or public conversations with Vasalians.

As already mentioned, white supremacy in the economic, political, social, and socioeconomic realms is unremarkable and thus constitutes doxa. Orthodox discourses are explanations that attempt to restore the invisibility of doxa, or white privilege. Bourdieu defines orthodoxy as "straight or rather *straightened* opinion, which aims, without ever entirely succeeding, at restoring the primal innocence of doxa, exists only in the objective relationship it opposes to heterodox, that is by reference to choice."

Heterodoxy, an alternative discourse to that of the orthodoxic discourse, is defined by Bourdieu as "*heresies,* heresy, made possible by the existence of competing possibilities" (1977, 169). My suggestion that racial inequality is responsible for the absence of a black elite constitutes a heterodoxic discourse in Vasalia, an alternative to doxa, that is, the ideology of racial democracy. Discourses that fail to restore the invisibility of white privilege constitute *heterodoxic* discourses. Vasalians turned to orthodoxic discourses when asked to account for the whiteness of the elite.

Orthodoxy: Discourses of Class Inequality, Inheritance, *Mestiçagem*

In this section I will map the orthodoxic responses that Vasalians employed to defend against my suggestions of a heterodoxic, or heretical discourse—that of racism. These defensive discourses enable Vasalians to avoid recognizing racial inequality as an explanation for the whiteness of the elite.

I have already noted that white supremacy in the aesthetic, economic, political, social, and religious realms is assumed in Vasalia. When directly asked to comment upon the concentration of Afro-Brazilians in positions of manual labor, virtually every resident interviewed attributed this absence to *class* inequality. I found no discursive differences between Afro- and Euro-Brazilians in response to the question "How would your life be different if you were [a different color]?" Rosana Heringer, a Brazilian scholar, argues:

> The main problem that the Black Movement has in its struggle against racism in Brazil is that many Black people do not recognize their unfavorable situation in Brazilian society as due to racial discrimination, inequality or prejudice. Many Blacks do not see racial discrimination because they live in a society where about 60% of the workforce, including White and non-White people, receives no more than U.S. $200 monthly salary. . . . It is difficult to notice racial discrimination amid what appears to be universal poverty. (1995, 205)

This problem is not restricted to working-class Brazilians. In his analysis of the responses of Afro-Brazilians university students to acts of social discrimination in the late 1970s, J. Michael Turner (1985) also observed: "When acts of social discrimination were admitted, the explanation supported by the students was that these occurrences were based upon class perceptions rather than upon racial identification. The person being discriminated against was perceived as being of the lower classes, not Afro-Brazilian: this class explanation was a precept dearly held by both students and nonstudents. Repeated questioning by foreign researchers would almost inevitably elicit the response that discrimination was based upon class."

This orthodoxic discourse is further illustrated by excerpts from an interview Jonathan Warren conducted with a Euro-Brazilian schoolteacher. When asked, "Does racism exist in Vasalia?" Sonia, a thirty-two-year-old teacher, responded:

Sonia Here in Vasalia, there is no racism.

JW There isn't any?

Sonia Nothing that I have observed.

JW Then why are the majority of the people of color poor?

Sonia Poor? In Vasalia?

JW In Vasalia. In Brazil.

FIGURE 13. The residence of two working-class Euro-Brazilian families. *(Photo by the author.)*

> *Sonia* In Brazil, the majority of the Brazilian population is poor. The minority has the power.
>
> *JW* But there are whites who are not poor.
>
> *Sonia* There are whites who aren't poor and there are blacks who aren't poor. Pelé, for example.
>
> *JW* How many black landowners do you know?
>
> *Sonia* That's a good question because I don't know a single one [anxious laughter].

Another example can be taken from Eliana, a forty-year-old Afro-Brazilian who describes herself as a mulatta. Her parents and several of her siblings continue to reside on the same plantation on which their slave ancestors lived. Neither of her parents received any formal education and consequently are illiterate. They receive no cash for their labor but instead live in a small house provided by the Luso-Brazilian landowner and farm a small piece of land. Eliana argues that racism is not a problem for people with money and shifts the discussion to class inequality. "I think that for the majority of people here, racism only occurs if someone has less money than them. I think that here . . . color means less here than the dollar. If a black person with a lot of money arrives, he will be treated like heaven. They will push him up higher. If he has an empty pocket, he won't be accepted. . . . Vasalians believe that whoever has money is superior. . . . Only money is important."

Even among Vasalians aware of racial discrimination, there was a tendency to identify socioeconomic status as the only significant factor in the life chances of Afro-Brazilians, while race was ignored. This is true for Miguel, a thirty-seven-year-old dark-skinned Vasalian who campaigned for a seat on the city council in 1992. Although he lost the election and described being devastated by this, Miguel never identified his dark skin color or racism as a factor in his defeat. While Miguel reported that in the past he had been called derogatory names such as *macaca* (monkey), he continued to frame his failure to win public office exclusively in terms of his socioeconomic status.

> I was a candidate for the city council but I lost. . . . I was the only black candidate. . . . In that time period, it was the worst period of my life because I was without money. . . . I ran my campaign by foot and by horse. Without money today, you resolve very few things in Brazil. I believe that if I had had money I would have been elected, but I am not upset because of this. I don't want to run anymore as a political candidate. I lost my will because a candidate for office has to have a little money.

Although class is obviously an important factor in the ability of a candidate to run an effective campaign, Miguel does not consider race as a possible additional factor in his failure to secure the votes he needed. In formal interviews and causal conversations, however, both Afro- and Euro-Brazilians said that they would not support a black candidate for the position of *vereador* (city council representative) because they didn't think that blacks possessed the skills or intelligence to be an effective politician. I was told repeatedly by white residents that they had heard other whites say that they "wouldn't vote for a monkey to represent them." Afro- and Euro-Brazilians reported to me that blacks weren't elected to public office because they weren't interested in being on the city council.

When denying the existence of racism, Vasalians would point to the existence of poor whites as evidence that there is no racism in their commu-

nity because a significant number of Euro-Brazilians have the same socioeconomic status as Afro-Brazilians. Like the working-class Afro-Brazilians,
when working-class Euro-Brazilians are asked about racism they also *shift*
the discussion to the shared plight of poor and working-class people who occupy the same socioeconomic status. Note how Alessandro, a thirty-three-
year-old Italian-Brazilian pharmacy owner of poor origins deracializes himself
and explains class dynamics. "In school, I used to always feel that there was
a division—not by color but based upon the question of economic power. The
people of a higher economic status, I used to notice that they always remained
separated from the poorer people. On this basis, I was discriminated against
[as a poor white]."

Allesandro interprets the discrimination he experienced as a poor Euro-
Brazilian by middle-class Euro-Brazilians as evidence that socioeconomic status, not race, is the significant axis of power. The social segregation between
Euro-Brazilians of different socioeconomic classes is interpreted by working-class Euro-Brazilians to mean that Afro-Brazilians are also rejected on
the basis of their subordinate class position. Thus, the class position
of Afro-Brazilians is privileged while color and racial location is typically
minimized.

This interpretation is reinforced by the tendency of poor Euro-Brazilians
to avoid embracing or claiming a white identity. Working-class Euro-
Brazilians I came to know rarely, if ever, self-identified as white but typically described themselves as moreno. In contrast to their working-class
counterparts in the United States, they usually emphasized what they shared
with Afro-Brazilians.

Writing of the need to develop an effective antiracist strategy in Britain, Stuart Hall argues that ideologies are not isolated concepts but constitute a part of a larger worldview.

> In liberal ideology, "freedom" is connected with individualism and
> the "free" market. In socialist ideology, "freedom" is a collective con-
> dition, dependent on, not counterposed to "equality of condition,"
> as it is in liberal ideology. The same concept is differently positioned
> within the logic of different ideological discourses. One of the ways
> in which ideological struggle takes place and ideologies transformed
> is by articulating the elements differently, thereby producing a dif-

ferent meaning, breaking the chain in which they are currently fixed
(e.g., democratic = Free West). (1981, 28)

Applying Hall's argument to Vasalia, we see that for working-class Brazilians there is a conceptual link between racism and the existence of white
poverty. Thus, the logic is that if race were a primary axis of power and privilege, there would be no class of poor whites. Since substantial white poverty exists, Vasalians conclude that Afro- and Euro-Brazilians encounter the
same forms of social discrimination. The racial logic operating can be summarized as:

racism = absence of any class distinctions among whites
racism = all whites have access to material privilege and are thus
members of the middle classes
racism = whites are not subjected to social discrimination

Following Hall's prescription, Vasalians assume that if racism existed,
all whites would have access to middle-class privilege and status. For Afro-
Brazilians who follow this logic, white poverty must thus be conceptually
divorced from the question of whether Afro-Brazilians are subjected to racism if they are to generate a conceptual framework that can account for both
class oppression and racism.

At least one variation on the class inequality discourse is that of *inheritance.* When I questioned their characterizations of Vasalia as being free of
racial inequality with questions such as "Do you know any Afro-Brazilian
landowners of significance?" Vasalians typically replied "No." I would press
them to explain further. A typical response given by the Afro-Brazilians (mulattos, negros/pretos) interviewed cited inheritance. For example, Jorge, a
twenty-two-year-old Afro-Brazilian, responds to the question "Why do you
think that the elite in this city is almost exclusively white?":

Once again I don't know how to respond to you. But you're right.
They're all white. Perhaps it's a coincidence. . . . I think that this has
a lot to do with one's ancestors. Understand? Those families that are
wealthy are the descendants of wealthy people. Everything is inherited [white elites] inherited everything and they're going to continue
to inherit. In the past who owned the plantations? The owners of the
plantations were all whites. . . . And that's going to continue from

father to son, from father to son, from father to son. So that's how it happened and how it's going to continue.

These explanations obviously do not account for the upward mobility experienced by the descendants of very poor Italians who immigrated to this community three generations ago in the latter half of the nineteenth century. Allesandro, the great-grandson of one of these Italian immigrants, did *not* inherit his property from his ancestors. He purchased his business from the daughter of a Portuguese plantation owner. Another example of an Italian-Brazilian who experienced significant upward mobility within three generations is Dr. Giovanni. He is the medical director and cofounder of the local hospital who spent three years building a sixteen-room house, and did not inherit most of his wealth.[1]

Mestiçagem

Latin American scholars have argued that a discourse of *mestiçagem* (race mixture) makes public discussions of racism seem irrelevant (Skidmore [1974] 1993; Wade 1993). In a study of blacks in Colombia, British anthropologist Peter Wade observed, "The ideology of mixedness is flexible enough to encompass claims that the past is a history of mixture which has undone any racial or ethnic purity. Hence blacks are the same as everyone else and have no grounds for complaint since they suffer no discrimination as blacks. Challenges to inequality are thus defused, while discrimination is legitimated" (1993, 162).

The discourse of mestiçagem is linked to another discourse—one of Brazilian racial exceptionalism. Michael Hanchard argues that although the myth of racial democracy is beginning to erode, the ideological construct, which he calls "racial exceptionalism," remains a powerful ideological obstacle to Afro-Brazilian antiracist activism. "My conceptualization of racial exceptionalism reflects an attempt to explain the subtle ideological shift from the common sense belief that Brazil is a country without racial antagonisms to a qualified recognition of racial prejudice, discrimination, and subordination as a feature of Brazilian life, while maintaining the belief that relative to other multiracial polities Brazil is indeed a more racially and culturally accommodating society" (1994, 43).

This discourse of mestiçagem *shifts* the discussion away from racism and racial inequality by arguing that color/race is not a significant axis of privilege. Furthermore, it *deracializes* the white elite by arguing that the elite is not really white but brown because brunettes and morenos constitute the numerical majority of the people.

In Vasalia, this ideology of mestiçagem is employed when the ideology of class inequality fails to explain adequately the whiteness of the elite. Vasalians consistently argued that "we're all [racially] mixed—all morenos, so we can't be racist." In response to the question "How would you define racism?" Eduardo, a brown-skinned Afro-Brazilian police officer, says, "Here in Brazil, I think that here in Brazil there is less racism than in other countries, because here there is a general mixture of the races."

This discourse usually emerged in interviews with working-class Vasalians. For example, when I asked why all of the *vereadors* (city council representatives) are white, Afro-Brazilians would typically correct me and argue that there is a moreno on the city council. They would also argue that I didn't understand the color classification system. But middle-class and elite Vasalians always counteridentified this individual as a branco, confirming that, in their opinion (and mine), there were no *pessoas de cor* (people of color) on the city council. In contrast to working-class Vasalians, the elite used less expansive and restrictive criteria in calculating who is moreno or branco. They appeared less interested in convincing me that the elite is not exclusively white.

Demographic Defense: Whites Are the Majority

Another discourse that Vasalians offer in response to the question "How do you explain that in this community all of the elites are white?" is that whites constitute the *numerical* majority in this community therefore it is logical that they would predominate among the elites. This acknowledges the whiteness of the elite but does not recognize white racial privilege because it interprets the absence of nonwhites as a consequence of demography. A thirty-eight-year-old Italian-Brazilian schoolteacher offered such an argument after initially having difficulty generating an explanation for the disproportionate number of whites who occupy privileged positions in all spheres of Vasalian life. When asked "How many black teachers are there in Vasalia?" Vera responded:

There is one, two. . . . Let me see. I think that we have one. I am trying to say that . . . if we don't have more [black teachers] it is not because there is racism. I believe that this is not because racism exists here. I do not know how to explain this well. . . . Look, but I think that everyone is free to become a teacher. I think that there the paucity of black teachers is not a consequence of racism. . . . It is because the white population is larger here in Vasalia, understand?

If we consider the experiences of Ariana, who almost lost her position as the *sole* Afro-Brazilian teacher at her secondary school, we can see how problematic this account is. Informal racist practices that work to exclude Afro-Brazilians from various forms of employment are common. Here Ariana describes the *racismo cordial* (polite racism) that she encountered as a teacher in a white school.

When I started teaching in the school, parents and some directors, people of high rank [whites], in positions at the school, didn't like it. They didn't want me to teach. They wanted me to do something *outside* of the classroom. First, they didn't know my work and then this [pointing to her skin color] was weighed the most. As time went by, when it was the end of the year, they had a meeting at the school . . . there were two very famous white teachers. And incredible as it seems, one of them, if it weren't for her, I wouldn't be at that school. She is not racist. Not all [whites] are. But if it weren't for her, I wouldn't have lasted until the end of the year. They would have kicked me out and put someone else in my place—very politely. Without anyone noticing. Without my becoming offended. But deep down, this is racial discrimination.

Despite Ariana's university training, teaching credentials, and competence in teaching literacy to students, attempts were made by white parents and administrators to remove her from the classroom because of her dark skin color.

Whites often express white supremacist ideologies toward Afro-Brazilian professionals in "polite" ways in Vasalia. For example, although the white administrators or parents didn't want her to teach because she is black, Ariana was never explicitly told that her race was a factor in this. However, as she reported, white parents went to the school administrators and complained about having a black person teaching their white children. Since Ariana's students were learning to read and write very quickly, the white school administrators were not easily able to dismiss her on the basis of her professional competence. Yet, in the end, it was not her competence but the intervention of white schoolteachers that enabled her to retain her job.

The comments of Ariana's father, Senhor Fernando, reflect the more typical and orthodox thinking that I found among Vasalians. He employed a demographic justification to explain the absence of Afro-Brazilians from the among the wealthy, privileged, and land-owning classes. "I believe it is because there are whites [in all of these positions], because of their numbers. This is the case in all of Brazil. The number of blacks is small. There are more whites than blacks so I think because of this that the elites are white. Because blacks are few [in number] and there are more whites."

This way of thinking strategically inflates the white population of Vasalia and thus normalizes white domination by deracializing the elite. The logic of this discourse enables Vasalians to argue that the elite does not represent a racialized group.[2] However, the absence of Afro-Brazilians in elected positions, land ownership, the priesthood, small business ownership, and their virtual exclusion from the professions is only rational if Euro-Brazilians constituted 100 percent of the Vasalian population.

According to the official census figures for this region, which includes Vasalia as one of several satellites of the city of Boa Vista, brancas officially constitute approximately 60 percent of the population. If we accept these federal census figures as an accurate reflection of the socially recognized white population, then at least one Afro-Brazilian should be among the economic and political elite. Instead, Vasalians were unable to identify a single Afro-Brazilian or person of color in the ranks of the elites.

Discourse of Cultural Inferiority

In her research among working-class Afro-Brazilians living in an urban *morro*[3] Robin Sheriff, a U.S. white anthropologist, found a discourse around racism that she describes as a "suppressed transcript." Sheriff says that "[Afro-Brazilians] thus participate to a certain degree in a discourse that in effect, denies or masks the social reality of racism. . . . They engaged in an everyday discourse that articulates and supports the notion that *negros* are in many senses, inferior to whites."

I found a similar discourse that I refer to as one of *cultural inferiority* among Afro-Brazilians. It typically emerged in public jokes among Vasalians and in private conversations with Afro-Brazilians when other discourses failed adequately to explain the absence of Afro-Brazilians from the elite. The argument that dark-skinned Afro-Brazilians are culturally inferior to Euro-Brazilians appeared to be shared among all segments of Vasalian society, including dark-skinned Afro-Brazilians who self-identify as negro or preto. I was surprised when Fernando, a sixty-seven-year-old self-identified negro trained in law and owner of a gas station, responds to my question about the absence of a black middle class or elite.

> *FWT* Could you explain why poor Italian immigrants have been able to experience upward mobility within two or three generations while Afro-Brazilians, as a group, have experience no significant upward mobility in this region?
>
> *Fernando* I understand your question. We don't have many poor Italians anymore. It's because the foreigners [pause]. It's not because blacks earn less. It's because foreigners save more. Do you know what I mean? To save. . . . It's not always the person who earns the most that is the richest. But the richest is that person who economizes the most. So the Italians, the strangers that came to Brazil, even though they were poor, they economized more [. . .] and the Africans who came to Brazil . . . For example, there in Africa, they had blacks of a higher class, but the blacks who immigrated to Brazil, [the Portuguese] took from those African tribes [slaves] that were the most backward, primitive, and that brought that type of behavior here with them . . . so they didn't have the facility to progress like the Italians.

Jorge, an Afro-Brazilian, responds in a similar fashion when asked "How would you explain the fact that all of the bank employees are white?": "I think that it must be because of this. Blacks haven't been able to obtain those jobs because they lack intelligence/knowledge. Their I.Q. is not high enough to get the job. It must be because of their I.Q. because they have the opportunity, because the exams are open to everyone. In the state of Rio, it's an open exam. If a black passes the exam, he is hired. Blacks are not pre-vented from taking the bank exam."

A similar line of argument has been described by Thomas Skidmore as having its origin in Brazilians' belief in both white supremacy and "exceptional" blacks. Skidmore says that "there is just enough upward mobility for Negroes and especially mulattos to sustain the argument that failure to rise is a consequence of individual *inadequacy* and not [racial] discrimination. Negroes themselves sometimes indicate their disbelief in the existence of prejudice" ([1974] 1993, 217).

These conceptualizations enable Vasalians to manage the gap between their ideal of racial egalitarianism and the exclusion of Afro-Brazilians from the ranks of the economically and socially privileged. This analytical framework shifts their focus from an emphasis upon *individual* achievement and ability to the abilities of *racial* groups reminiscent of theories of scientific racism.

It is more difficult to explain Fernando's comments since he self-identifies as a preto and thus belongs to the group that he argues is the most backward in Brazil. Since racial segregation is de facto and not absolute, a handful of well-educated Afro-Brazilians are marginally involved in the pro-fessional life of the middle-class Euro-Brazilians, although even this level of integration is clearly superficial, like the one black in a bank of twenty workers that Ariana reported.

Discourses of Containment: Temporal

Frequently, Vasalians deployed discourses to *contain* racism either spa-tially or temporally, to explain why racism has no impact upon their personal life in Vasalia. These discourses of containment can be defined as discursive strategies used to marginalize racism or deem it irrelevant to one's life by locating racism in another temporal moment or geographical space that is outside of one's immediate milieu.

In his schematic mapping of several of the conflicting "racial projects" that constituted racial hegemony in the United States in the 1980s, Howard Winant delineates one racial discourse, *neoconservatism*, which may also de-scribe how the invisibility of white racial privilege is defended in Vasalia. In this discourse of neoconservatism, racism is defined as "a vestige of the past, when invidious distinctions and practices had not yet been reformed" (1994, 31). Like fairy tales with happy endings, some of the Afro-Brazilians interviewed claimed that racism had ended in 1888 when Princessa Isabella signed the law abolishing slavery, while others said that it ended twenty-five years ago when it "became inconvenient."

Until 1986, all of the stores on the main street in Boa Vista, where Vasalians do their shopping, had been segregated by race. Ariana, the daughter of Fernando, the sole black lawyer and the only highly educated Afro-Brazilian in this community, reported that as recently as 1985 even the sidewalks of the main street were segregated by color. When asked "Can you provide any specific examples of racism?" several Afro-Brazilian men described in detail the Jim Crow–like segregation of the main street, stores, public sidewalks, social clubs, dances, and beauty contests that had been in practice up to 1985, saying in private "that happened a long time ago."[4] White Vasalians also reluctantly confessed, also in private, that public segregation by skin color and race had occurred as recently as seven years ago. Racism is contained by both Afro- and Euro-Vasalians within a larger narrative of "progress" in Vasalia. Camillo, an Afro-Brazilian, describes his childhood of racial segregation as evidence that racism is not a problem in Vasalia *today*.

> *Camillo* When I was a child [1975], I was nine years old, there was [racial] segregation here. People of color were not allowed to enter the swimming pools, the clubs. They did not use the term *negro* then. They used to say *pessoas de cor*.
>
> *JW* Here in Vasalia? There were clubs for whites only?
>
> *Camillo* Yes. There used to be a club called the Club of Thirteen. During the time that the club existed I was nine years old. The club closed by the time I was ten years old. Blacks were perceived by whites as bad people. And among the majority of blacks that I know, there are only a few good ones . . . so the families of my grandfather's time did not accept interracial socializing. [Whites] believed that [blacks] were like dogs, like animals because the [blacks] did not know how to behave themselves, understand?

Later in the interview, Camillo argued that today blacks and whites go to the "same social events," so racism is not a contemporary feature of social life.

Henrique, a forty-three-year-old dark-skinned Afro-Brazilian, also juxtaposes the Jim Crow–like racial segregation of the past with evidence that racism does not exist today.

> For example, the club was called the Elite. It was exclusively for whites. People of color were not allowed to enter. In our region, in the *old days*, there were such things. It was discrimination based upon skin color and not social class. In some places around here . . . if you were black regardless of your ability to pay, you would be prohibited from entering. [The whites] would not allow you to enter. . . . But in the past, some fifteen or twenty years ago, this type of discrimination used to occur regularly.

In Henrique's narrative, racism is located in another *temporal* moment. Racist incidents that occurred in the past are offered as proof that racism does not exist in contemporary life.

A related discursive strategy used by Afro-Brazilians to contain racism and locate it as outside of their milieu involves defining people who engage in overt acts of racism today as belonging to the past. This can be seen in Jorge's comments: "For example, sometimes racism exists here among *very old* people. For example, in the case of my grandparents, who told stories about how the plantation owners used to prohibit blacks from entering their homes. Blacks had to remain in the slave quarters. [Whites] didn't want to mix with them. . . . Blacks were not allowed inside of their houses, no! Blacks had to eat outside. . . . Now today we don't have racism anymore because blacks can enter the kitchen and eat in the homes of whites."

Discourses of Containment: Spatial

Vasalians often described what can be called a form of spatial apartheid that they encountered in the city of Rio. This racial and class segregation is reflected in the design of apartment buildings and hotels in elite neighborhoods. The spatial geography of urban Rio bears some striking similarities to the Jim Crow southern United States. There is a *social* entrance, reserved for building residents and guests who are presumed to be white, and a *service* entrance, located at the side or the back of these buildings, for the exclusive use of domestic maids and service providers, who are presumed to be nonwhite or black. In an analysis of published reports of racism in forty urban newspapers, Brazilian sociologist Antonio Sérgio Alfredo Guimarães describes this form of racism: "It is interesting to observe that the denial of access or the embarrassment suffered by black visitors who want access to residential buildings, follows the same logic as the restriction of the right to circulate which I [noted] previously. It is a case in which people are considered suspect based on their color . . . color here is only a signifier of *social origin*, in other words, an attributed status, thus all blacks are suspect" (1996).[5]

When asked to describe racism, Vasalians often described highly publicized cases of this type of racism involving a black journalist or more often a North American or foreign black being denied access to a hotel or luxury building. They would confidently emphasize that this would never occur in Vasalia, but only in the larger coastal cities of Rio de Janeiro and São Paulo. I would remind them that there are no luxury buildings in Vasalia so there are no opportunities to engage in this practice. Ironically, when I visited Rio to change money, visit the library, and obtain documents, I would be told by the cariocas that racism is much worse in the small cities in the interior of the state.

In an article entitled "Small Cities Also Have Racism" published in June 1995 as part of a special supplement on "Racismo Cordial" by the *Jornal do São Paulo*, the largest newspaper in Brazil's largest city, the authors wrote: "One of the current assumptions is that there is less racial prejudice in small cities, because of the closer relations between people. But Datafolha proved that this is not true. Residents of small cities display racist feelings in identical proportion to medium and large size cities."[6]

When giving examples of racism, the Vasalians would typically shift their discussion to larger metropolitan communities outside of Vasalia. The Afro- and Euro-Brazilians would talk of incidents that had occurred in *other* cities, states, or nations. Eduardo, a twenty-one-year-old brown-skinned Afro-Brazilian who works as a military police officer, responds to a question about racism.

> I think that in the U.S. the blacks feel oppressed. They feel stepped on by the whites. The whites push blacks around. And here that doesn't happen. People here don't pay attention to [race]. If a person wants to accomplish something, whether they are black or white, they can succeed. [In the United States], there is a difference in the treatment that whites and blacks receive. [North Americans] give preference to the white over the blacks. Here that doesn't happen. It is a question of the capacity of the person. Be it employment or politics.

In private conversations, Euro-Brazilians engaged in the same discursive practice. For example, in private conversation with Lorenzo, the blond, blue-eyed, recently elected mayor of Vasalia, he responded to the question "Does racism exist in Vasalia?" by asserting, "No. . . . I saw a case [on television], for example, involving the daughter of the [black] governor of Espirito Santo. (She was subjected to racism.) I was profoundly saddened by this news. Thank God, Espirito Santo is a long way from here. In our town, thank God, we don't have this problem. I would be the first to punish this type of racism."

The mayor shifts the discussion to another geographical space, to a highly publicized incident in which the nineteen-year-old Afro-Brazilian daughter of the Afro-Brazilian governor of the adjacent state of Espirito Santo had been physically held and assaulted by a Euro-Brazilian woman and her son in an elevator. Espirito Santo is positioned in his narrative as a "long way from here," when in fact it is less than a thirty-minute drive by car. Vasalians are further linked to towns in Espirito Santo through marriage alliances, vacation rituals, and friendship networks. The beaches of Espirito Santo are a favorite destination spot for the town elites, who leave during the Carnival season since there is no Carnival parade held in Vasalia in February. Espirito Santo is an integral part of the social world of elite Vasalians. The mayor, a Euro-Brazilian elite, who has four Afro-Brazilian live-in domestic servants, supports the official public discourse of racial egalitarianism by emphasizing the difference between Vasalia and cities in other states. He, like the Afro-Brazilians interviewed, located racism outside of Vasalia, and outside of the normative experience of its residents.

If we compare the comments of Afro- and Euro-Brazilians in response to these questions, no significant differences emerge. An example of the prevalence of this discourse of spatial containment is reflected in the comments of Margarida, a nineteen-year-old Afro-Brazilian, who said that although "some" racism existed in Brazil she had "never observed any racism in Vasalia." Like the mayor, she discusses racism as something that she only has access to through national television news reports. Racism is marginal to her personal experiences in Vasalia. "There have been cases of racism that appeared on the television. A black female journalist was not allowed to enter a fashionable place in the city of Rio. She was a journalist and prosecuted the guy. Then this event received a lot of commentary. That happened there [in Rio]. Here in our city, you will not see much racism. You see that people treat other people in a normal manner."

Isabela, an upper-class Euro-Brazilian small business owner in Vasalia, also shifts the discussion to another urban context. She had lived in the city of Rio for more than seven years and had returned to Vasalia after a failed marriage. Like several of her cousins, after her first marriage failed, she returned home to Vasalia. She subsequently married a man whom she met while on vacation in a town in Espirito Santo. Notice how Isabela shifts the discussion to the city of Rio in response to the question "Can you provide an example of racism?":

Isabela When I lived in Rio, I used to work at a center for data processing, a computer firm. And we used to receive quite a few résumés for job openings. I used to file the résumés. We could not determine from the names, if the persons who sent the résumés were black. We didn't know if they were black or white because we couldn't see them, right? We only saw the skills that they had, understand? And when the applicants were called for interviews based upon the résumés they submitted, I always used to think that there was a certain amount of discrimination against blacks. So much so that in the company I worked for, the only position that blacks held were as office boys.

FWT They only worked as office boys?

Isabela That's right. Among the real bosses, there were no blacks. Not a single black supervisor. And in the data processing center there used to be only one mulatto, he was the computer programmer. Only one. The rest were all white. Not one black, there were four floors. It was a company business. And on each floor there were twenty offices. . . . Also when I worked in aviation industry, I never saw a

black pilot. Never. I used to work with many pilots and what do you
call them, airline stewardesses. I never saw a black airline stewardess.

After describing the exclusion of blacks from several different companies, Isabela characterizes the exclusion as *exceptional* and unique to the metropolitan companies she worked for in Rio. She does not acknowledge that
these same practices may also occur in Vasalia. She does not appear to perceive any parallels or links between the absence of Afro-Brazilians in positions in firms in the City of Rio and their absence in the banks of Vasalia.

Vasalians do not consider the consequences of informal, subtle, coded,
or unconscious practices that deny employment access to Afro-Brazilians but
only consider formally declared, and *state-sanctioned* prohibitions. Thus, few
residents perceived the absence of Afro-Brazilians as employees in the local
bank, post office, or other institutions as noteworthy or indicative of racial
inequality.

When racism cannot be entirely denied as a feature of contemporary
Brazilian life, it can be contained by its definition as a problem located *outside* of their local community. Vera, a thirty-eight-year-old Italian-Brazilian
schoolteacher reiterated this strategy and extended it to argue that common-
alities, not differences, united Vasalians. When asked "Do you think that poor
blacks encounter the same problems as poor whites in Brazil?" Vera replies:

> Listen, I don't know [about racism] because here in Vasalia, there is
> one reality and in the bigger cities there is a different reality. Here
> in Vasalia, poor people, beggars don't exist like they have in Rio de
> Janeiro. I think that here in Vasalia everyone encounters the same
> problems. They could be whites. They could be black. I am trying
> to say that if there are difficulties, the difficulties are for both races.
> We see a lot of reports on television. For example, in Rio the major-
> ity of the problems that occur generally affect persons of a darker
> skin color. They encounter most of the problems. What I am trying
> to say is that here there is one reality and in the big cities there is
> another reality. I don't see the problems of racism here.

Like other Brazilians interviewed, Vera places racism outside of Vasalian
life by contrasting it with the city of Rio de Janeiro. She also describes racism as something that she experiences only from a distance—from televi-

sion. Her knowledge of racism comes from events outside the local community. It is not a defining part of the reality of dark-skinned people in her community. Instead, the "one reality" of Vasalia leaves no place for the recognition of the visible signs of racism.

Ariana, an Afro-Brazilian teacher who had grown up in Boa Vista until her marriage to Miguel eight years ago, is more critical of Vasalia. Her descriptions of local institutions contradict the benign image of racial egalitarianism presented by natives of Vasalia such as Vera and Isabela. The demographics described by Ariana suggest that in Vasalia, as in businesses in the larger city of Rio, Afro-Brazilians do not have desirable positions, especially positions involving working with the public.

> *Ariana* It is unusual for [a black] to enter a bank. . . . BANERJ is the bank of the state of Rio de Janeiro. Only one black has been able to get a job [in the local branch of this bank]. And until today it is only him.
>
> *FWT* How many employees are working at this bank?
>
> *Ariana* Ah! There must be at least twenty.
>
> *FWT* And here in Vasalia?
>
> *Ariana* I have never seen a black working in the bank here. And I can count on my fingers . . . how many blacks even have bank accounts.

In contrast to all of the other Vasalians interviewed, Ariana considers the *absence* of Afro-Brazilians from positions as salesclerks and bank tellers a valid measure of racism. She explicitly identifies this absence as a consequence of informal racist practices. More typical among native Vasalians is an emphasis on formal, legal, and state-sanctioned prohibitions (those forms most common under U.S. Jim Crow and South African apartheid). The only residents who pointed to the absence of absence of Afro-Brazilians were individuals who had married into the community but had been born and raised outside of Vasalia.

Conclusion

In this chapter I analyzed the discourses that Vasalians use to rationalize the virtual absence of Afro-Brazilians from the ranks of the elite. These discourses enable Vasalians to counter my suggestions that racism is partially responsible for the subordinate group position of Afro-Brazilians in Vasalia. They also enable Vasalians to strategically manage the social and material inequality that exists between Afro-Brazilians and Euro-Brazilian elites. This is accomplished by employing arguments that *deracialize* the elite, thereby restoring the invisibility of their whiteness and thus of white racial privilege.

These discourses are particularly important for Afro-Brazilians because they must conceptually manage information that could potentially call attention to white domination. In addition, they also maintain the innocence of the elite and the upwardly mobile Afro-Brazilians because, as sociologist Carlos Hasenbalg maintains, "This official racial ideology produced a feeling of relief among the whites, who could then regard themselves as exempt from *any* responsibility toward the social problems of blacks and mulattos" (Hasenbalg 1996; see also Hasenbalg 1978). In Vasalia, it is not only whites but Afro-Brazilians who may be relieved because they can maintain the fiction that once they have achieved a degree of socioeconomic mobility they will not be subjected to racial discrimination.

I employed Bourdieu's concepts of doxa, orthodoxy, and heterodoxy as a framework for understanding how racial disparities are rationalized among Brazilians who sustain their faith that they live in a democracia racial. I found that the orthodoxic discourse, that is the discourse of "choice" for explaining the inequality between Afro- and Euro-Brazilians, is one of class inequality. This discourse *deracializes* the Euro-Brazilian elite by privileging socioeconomic status as the primary axis of power. I mapped several defensive discourses Vasalians employ to avoid recognizing white supremacy. These orthodoxic discourses attempt to maintain the invisibility of white privilege by defining racism as a phenomenon located outside the temporal and spatial domain of Vasalians. By shifting the discussion to incidents that occur outside their community, Vasalians defend dominant conceptions of social reality that sustain racial harmony and white supremacy.

CHAPTER 5

Embranquecimento: Aesthetic Ideals and Resistance to Mestiçagem

For several years certain laboratories have been trying to produce a serum for "denegrification," with all the earnestness in the world, laboratories have . . . embarked on research that might make possible for the miserable Negro to whiten himself and thus throw off the burden of that corporeal malediction.
—Frantz Fanon (1967, 111)

I say that the Black masses in Brazil have only one option: to disappear. Whether it be through compulsory miscegenation assimilation or, when they escape this, through direct elimination—death pure and simple. This has been going on for four centuries.
—Abdias do Nascimento ([1979] 1987, 7)

If we admit that Negroes and Indians are continuing to disappear, both in the successive dilutions of white blood and in the constant process of biological and social selection . . . the white man will not only have in Brazil his major field of life and culture in the tropics, but be able to take from old Europe—citadel of the white race—before it passes to other hands, the torch of western civilization to which Brazilians will give a new and intense light.
—Fernando de Azevedo, quoted in Thomas Skidmore ([1974] 1993, 208)

$\mathcal{T}$he ideology of *embranquecimento* (whitening), and the concomitant practice of *mestiçagem* (race mixture), has been described by numerous scholars as a primary pillar of white supremacy in Latin America (Skidmore 1974; Wright 1990; Wade 1993). The "whitening ideology" was originally coined by the Brazilian elite to reconcile theories of scientific racism with the reality of the predominantly nonwhite population of their country. The elite formulated a unifying national ideology that would convince themselves that Brazil could, despite its disadvantaged racial stock, be transformed in to a modern nation.

> The Brazilian theory of "whitening," . . . coming to be accepted by most of the Brazilian elite during the years between 1889 and 1914, was a theory peculiar to Brazil. Seldom stated as "scientific" formula and certainly never embraced in Europe or North America, it is worth explaining here in some detail.
>
> The whitening thesis was based on the assumption of white superiority—sometimes muted by leaving open the question of how "innate" the inferiority might be and using the euphemisms "more advanced" and "less advanced" races. But to this assumption were added two more. First, the black population was becoming progressively less numerous than the white for reasons which included a supposedly lower birth rate, higher incidence of disease, and social disorganization. Second, miscegenation was "naturally" producing a lighter population, in part because white genes were stronger and in part because people chose partners lighter than themselves. (Skidmore [1974] 1993, 64–65)

In this chapter, I explore embranquecimento, an ideology and practice embraced by Afro-Brazilians in Vasalia. Although interracial relationships are legitimated and publicly sanctioned in Brazil by a national discourse of mestiçagem, we cannot assume that this practice does not meet with some resistance among whites who may not want to include Afro-Brazilians in their families of reproduction.

This chapter asks if the ideology of embranquecimento and the practice of mestiçagem are equally embraced by Vasalians. If not, who contests or resists mestiçagem and under what conditions do they do so? (The current body of ethnographic literature on Brazilian race relations gives little empirical data about resistance to mestiçagem.) Finally, how does this practice of embranquecimento intersect with and thereby reinforce white supremacy in Brazil?

The Racial Hierarchy of Desirability: The White Ideal

The mass media in Brazil, particularly television, reflects and reinforces the practice of embranquecimento by idealizing Brazilians who possess blond hair, light-colored eyes, and other markers of European ancestry. Like Amelia Simpson, I found that television is a primary source of information, entertainment, and education in Brazil. According to Simpson, "Brazilians watch more television than any other third-world people. The nation ranks fourth in the world in the number of television sets (28 million), behind only the United States (154 million), Japan (79 million) and Britain (33 million)" (1993, 43). My research in Vasalia suggests that in rural communities, television is the single most important source of education.[1] In rural areas and very poor households, a television will be found in households that lack a refrigerator, bed, or telephone (Scheper-Hughes 1992).

Employing Richard Dyer's concept of the "racial hierarchy of desirability," Amelia Simpson analyzes how white supremacist ideologies circulate on Brazil's most popular television program, the Xuxa show:

> Xuxa's promotion of a white ideal invests the old message of the superiority of whiteness with extraordinary power in the age of mass media. She fits perfectly into a nearly universal mentality of privilege, one that endorses what Dyer calls the "racial hierarchy of desirability." Xuxa's fair skin, blond hair, and blue eyes, and the replication of that look in the Paquitas and in the many products connected with the "Xou," reinforce what most people in Brazil learn about race from the time they are very young. These images circulate in the society at large, but are especially pervasive through the mass media and the advertising industry, which as, Carlos Hasenbalg has observed "reinforce the negative self-image of Brazilians who are either invisible or portrayed in stereotypical roles." Anybody who watches Brazilian television for half a day sees that it is dominated by whites and by white images of power, success, intelligence and beauty. (1993, 37–38)

The absence of black Brazilians on television in nonstereotypical roles is one mechanism by which Euro-Brazilians come to be defined as the aesthetic ideal. This ideal is promoted both through both the predominance of blond Euro-Brazilians in the mass media and the negative images of Afro-Brazilians and dark-skinned Brazilians. Telenovelas and shows such as Xuxa normalize this ideology through the exclusion of Afro-Brazilians from its representations of the middle class, the beautiful, and the powerful.

In an interview with two sisters from a multiracial family conducted by Daphne Patai, the white-skinned sister explains how white supremacist aesthetic hierarchies generate divisions within her own family of multiracial heritage.

> The hierarchy's like this: hair, nose, and mouth, these are the three major things—and skin color afterward. I've always noticed this in Brazil, I think it's a result of miscegenation, specific to this country. What has left the deepest mark in terms of negative views of Blacks, in practical terms, is really this business of the mouth, thick lips, the flat nose, the kinky hair. If Julia didn't have kinky hair, if it were straight, she'd never be identified as having Negro ancestry, right, Julia? No, because she's morena. In our household we have a living example of this situation, of how it makes people. . . . For example, we live together, but at first people never believe we're sisters. Despite all the miscegenation in this country, people don't openly admit it. We've learned how to deal with it, and we have to, to this day. . . . Just look at the prejudice in my own family. They're very racist; they discriminate against their own brothers and sisters. For example, my great-aunt, my grandmother's sister, is Black, and she used to say that Augusto's mother had a "dirty womb," because all her children were mulatto or Black. This made a very strong impression on me as a child. (Patai 1988, 13)

When asked for descriptions of their aesthetic ideal, this same aesthetic hierarchy of desirability emerged in conversations with Vasalians. Children and adults expressed a strong aesthetic preference for individuals who possessed features typically associated with European ancestry. Unexpectedly, I found that Afro-Brazilians were more likely than Euro-Brazilians to explicitly articulate this aesthetic hierarchy in their descriptions of who they found particularly attractive. The overvaluation of features such as white skin, light eyes, light hair, and straight hair is articulated through the repetitive and seemingly unselfconscious desire for and adoration of Vasalians who possess these traits. The following quotations taken from private taped conversations illustrate the valorization of whiteness by Vasalians of all backgrounds.

Tatiana, a fifty-one-year-old Afro-Brazilian *dona de casa* (homemaker) married to a dark-skinned black man, describes why Afro-Brazilians express a strong preference for lighter-skinned or white Brazilians as their spouses: "It is to have *more beautiful* children, more beautiful grandchildren. The parents do this in order to have more beautiful children. To have [children with] hair that does not require much work to keep it neat, because straight hair is much easier, isn't it? There are many [black] people that prefer white spouses. My [black] father-in-law, the father of [my black husband] prefers that his children marry whites."

Margarida, a light-skinned eighteen-year-old Afro-Brazilian student, describes the men who she finds desirable: "I *adore blonds that have blue eyes* and muscles. I adore these types of people. . . . It is very difficult to define beauty, isn't it? Every person has their own beauty but I really like tall people, prefer blonds, with straight hair."

Henrique, a forty-three-year-old dark-skinned Afro-Brazilian married to a white woman explains why he married a white woman: "[Blacks marry whites] because whites have good hair. [Whites] have good hair, their nose is not ugly [like ours]. Blacks normally have very large lips, like an animal's and people think this is ugly. I am trying to say that black people know that [their features] are ugly and white people also know that blacks are ugly."

Isabela, a thirty-four-year-old self-employed Euro-Brazilian business owner, says: "I have always liked light-skinned people, *blonds with blue eyes*. The majority of my lovers have looked like this, blonds with light eyes but I married a brunette with light eyes."

Raquel, a thirty-one-year-old Euro-Brazilian teacher with blond hair and blue eyes, who is married to a brunette, describes her ideal: "I consider a person beautiful if they are light-skinned . . . normally the features that attract me are white skin. . . . And usually *blonds attract my attention more*. And I think it is almost the same thing for a man, isn't it?"

Dr. Giovanni, a forty-one-year-old white medical doctor married to a woman with blond hair and blue eyes, notes:

It is difficult to speak of—to give a description of a beautiful person because there has been *too much racial mixture* here, right?. . . .

FIGURE 14. Neuza, daughter of Dona Rosaria, Jonathan Warren, and the author celebrating the birth of Nueza's son. Neuza's husband is a white policeman from the city of Rio de Janeiro. *(Photo by the author.)*

But what attracts me is a tall person with white skin, light eyes. I think that there are so many beautiful people! The ideal of beauty is a difficult business. We are more accustomed to describing physical beauty in terms of a white person . . . on the advertisements and the outdoor posters, there are always models of Scandinavian or German origins. They are all blondes with blue eyes. And this does not correspond with the physical type found in Brazil, does it? The type of woman that I naturally prefer is a tall woman, thin but not too thin, with *blond hair* also, thin and delicate nose, full lips. This is what the Brazilian man adores, right?

Moema, a thirty-four-year-old unmarried white woman, speaks of her feelings about beauty: "I think that the majority [of Blacks] reject people of their own color. . . . I think the problem is ours [white Brazilians] also because we always define someone beautiful as white. The wealthy person is white. The people that we socialize with the most are white. We [whites] reject black people and because of this, blacks reject themselves."

Tônica, a dark-skinned thirty-three-year-old Afro-Brazilian, describes her motivation for establishing a family with her domestic partner, a very poor Euro-Brazilian.

> *Tônica* Ah, no it's not that I felt better than blacks. But I used to talk to my mother like this: "Mother, when I get married I will marry a white man." My mother used to ask me, "Why?" I used to answer, "Because I don't want my children to be dark like me." You know? Then I used to think like this, I used to say that "If I found a white man to marry, that I would marry him, so that my kids would come out—so that they wouldn't be little darkies." So that means we also have [this problem of racism], right? . . . That just reminded me that many dark-skinned black men used to try to date me, but I wouldn't date them—no way. Why is that?
>
> *Husband* In this matter, only you know that.
>
> *Tônica* I don't even know. I don't even know why. I was really thinking of the children. I used to think, "OK, let me marry a person lighter than myself because if I marry a dark person like myself, [the children] are all going to be dark—the little children." But I was still thinking of the children, right? "So let me marry someone . . . if I found a lighter man . . . then I will marry a lighter man because then my children will come out prettier."

The above quotations from a range of Vasalians are typical of aesthetic ideals that stigmatize physical traits that signify African ancestry. I heard comments such as these every day in Vasalia. White skin, light and straight hair, light eyes (blue/green/hazel), and tall stature emerged as the dominant aesthetic ideals in Vasalia. Although not all Vasalians expressed an explicit aesthetic preference for whites, none argued for an alternative. Nor did they challenge this ideal that evaluates beauty on the basis of traits that reflect predominant European ancestry.

In casual conversations, Vasalians repeatedly described their aesthetic preferences in passionate detail, but they attempted to minimize the significance of these preference by statements such as "everyone has their own beauty" and "it is difficult to describe beauty."

Afro-Brazilian Resistance to Mestiçagem

I found no Afro-Brazilian resistance to the aesthetic hierarchies that I have outlined above. The Afro-Brazilians I interviewed and developed relationships with did not critique or challenge these hierarchies by arguing that they are as beautiful or more beautiful than whites. The only opposition that I found to mestiçagem was expressed by Ariana and Tatiana, two dark-skinned Afro-Brazilian women, both married to dark-skinned Afro-Brazilian men. Ariana, a teacher, and Tatiana, a dona da casa, challenged mestiçagem, but neither offered a sustained critique of these hierarchies.

Ariana was chemically straightening her hair when I arrived for our first scheduled life history interview. She rinsed her hair and began drying it as we moved into her bedroom. I had brought her copies of *Essence*, the U.S. black magazine, because she told me that she had *never* seen a Brazilian magazine that targeted black readers.[2] Ariana looked into the mirror and asked me why U.S. blacks are so much more beautiful than black Brazilians. Then she began to ask me if I could bring some hair relaxer for her daughter from the U.S. on my next trip back.[3] When I asked Ariana what her dreams were for her daughter, the first thing she said was that she wanted her daughter, whom she referred to as a preta, to marry a black man because marrying a white man would cause her too much pain.

> One dream would make me the happiest in my life. If and when my daughter marries, she marries a black. That's the dream of my life. . . . I am not going to discriminate (against whites). But what I don't want is her to suffer the consequences from this. . . . "Look at that black with that white man. There must be something [illicit] going on there." . . . Black, black, black, that's my daughter. So if she arrived with a white man, it is going to be a shock . . . she will suffer a lot of discrimination.

Ariana fears that her dark-skinned daughter, a preta, will be perceived as a prostitute, or, at best, a mistress, if she appears in public with a white man. She suggests that in Vasalia dark-skinned Afro-Brazilian women are not typically considered the legitimate social partners of white men, despite the public discourse of mestiçagem. When I asked Ariana if she knew of any middle-class whites married to Afro-Brazilians, she began laughing at me.

She looked at me as one looks at a child who has not grasped a basic concept of social life.

FWT Do you know any elite whites married to a black?

Ariana No.

FWT Is this common?

Ariana [Interracial marriage] isn't common here, or in any other place.

FWT Interracial marriage isn't common?

Ariana Involving an elite white?

FWT Yes, a wealthy white Brazilian?

Ariana To marry a black woman?[4] This would be news! It would be publicized.

FWT I've been told by many people that here [white] people like blacks, that they really like mulattas—that Brazilians are all racially mixed.

Ariana But who told you this? blacks[5] or whites?

FWT Mulattas and whites.

Ariana I know blacks with a social position, with money in their pocket looking for whites—for white girls. But whites who have social status, well-to-do, interested in black women? Have you ever heard of a case like that? He married her? He is white and married a black girl? Have you heard of that?

FWT No.

Ariana And you are *never* going to hear that! You could look around. Look around and you will see that. . . . Go anywhere and you will find out that this is difficult to find. Here in Vasalia a white man married a very dark-skinned girl. But they left here. They couldn't remain here and they went to Bom Jesus to get married and didn't return. When they come, he comes alone and she doesn't [visit her husband's family].

FWT Why doesn't she return with him?

Ariana Because she is a black.

Tatiana, a fifty-two-year-old dark-skinned Afro-Brazilian and the mother of four, is the only other Afro-Brazilian interviewed who expressed opposition to mestiçagem. Like Tatiana, she speaks from the position of a mother concerned about her children's suffering. She has a strong preference for her children to marry within their color group because of the humiliation they would encounter as members of a multiracial family. Tatiana explicitly identifies the potential abusive treatment by a white spouse who derives power from these aesthetic hierarchies. "I am not prejudiced against whites. In the hour of lovemaking, everything is wonderful. Afterwards, in the heat of a fight, I believe that the *first* thing that will be said [by the white partner] is "You black! You nigger! You monkey! . . . I have seen this occur in other [interracial] families. I know that this happens. I think that if my children would marry a person of their own color, they will not have these problems . . . everyone is not equal."

This can be read as a muted critique of the Brazilian racial democracy. What Tatiana is describing is the power differential between a black and white spouse. White partners, by virtue of their race, can use racial privilege and higher status as a weapon against their darker-skinned Afro-Brazilian partners. Tatiana does not want her children to be humiliated by a white partner because she recognizes the racial hierarchies involved in interracial marriages. Tatiana and Ariana were unique in explicitly recognizing and naming the "price" (for the Afro-Brazilian partner) of interracial marriages. Despite Tatiana's stated preference that her children marry within their color, all of her children had expressed strong preferences for whites and all were currently dating or married to whites at the time this interview was conducted.

Writing about the selection of partners by U.S. black women in the 1930s, U.S. white anthropologist Hortense Powdermaker wrote that North American black women cited the color gap (skin color differences) as one factor in the success of a marital relationship.

> Likes and dislikes are usually conceived of in terms of "lighter or darker than I am." . . . It is often deemed wise to avoid a great disparity in color. A minority of black skinned people preferred their own dark color in a mate. These are for the most part in the lower middle and lower class and the preference seems to arise from fear of feeling inferior to a lighter mate, or of being despised, or mistreated, or neglected and eventually deserted. On such a basis, even the negative preference implies the prestige of "white" traits and the disparagement of a Negroid appearance. . . . This was a very light woman, whose father was white and mother was half white. Her first husband was almost white and treated her badly. The next time she

FIGURE 15. Tônica, an empregada for a white elite family, and her husband, Sebastião. *(Photo by the author.)*

chose a man who was darker than she, and that marriage was more successful. She did not imply that color difference was the sole reason, but added that by the time of her second marriage, she was more experienced and could stand better what I had to do. . . . She feels that dark people do not care to associate with her as if she were black and that they do not treat her as well. (1939, 178)

As this excerpt from Powdermaker's ethnography suggests, during the pre–civil rights era U.S. blacks recognized that color differences (even among people who claim the same racial identity) can generate power differences. A delicate balance was negotiated by her informant between not selecting a partner who was too dark but not selecting one who was too light. In the context of the pre–civil rights era southern United States, black women considered skin color as one criterion in marriage, thus recognizing the realities of aesthetic hierarchies in North America.

Euro-Brazilian Resistance to Mestiçagem

Within a national context of the mestiçagem ideal and an aesthetic hierarchy that valorizes European ancestry, it is understandable that dark-skinned Brazilians of salient African ancestry prefer to date and marry lighter partners. One would also assume that in a racial democracy, whites would not reject Afro-Brazilians in marriage. How do Euro-Brazilians in Vasalia negotiate an aesthetic hierarchy that denigrates African ancestry amid the Afro-Brazilian practice of embranquecimento? In contrast to what I expected, there was a pattern of resistance to interracial marriage among Euro-Brazilians of all socioeconomic positions. Euro-Brazilians resisted mestiçagem by actively discouraging family members from establishing families with Vasalians of predominant or salient African ancestry.

Tônica, who describes herself as *escuro*, is from a poor family of coffee plantation workers, and has three children by her partner Sebastião, a white Brazilian from a very poor family of manual laborers. During a joint interview with her and her partner, Tônica describes the strong opposition that they faced when they announced their plans to marry twelve years ago.

Tônica When we were going to get married, many obstacles appeared.

The white relatives opposed it, because of my color, understand? Be-

FIGURE 16. Luisa, an aspiring Afro-Brazilian teacher, and her three sons. *(Photo by the author.)*

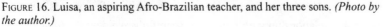

cause his relatives are white and my relatives are all blacks. So Sebastião's relatives began to interfere. But he didn't like anyone trying to stop his wedding so we got married.

FWT So sometimes poor whites have prejudices against blacks also?

Tônica Some do. There are rich people that do have *preconceito* (prejudice) against the poor and there are poor people that also do not like to be bothered with a person because they are black. So all of this [racism] occurs, not only with the rich, it also occurs with the poor whites.

Sebastião Like [my wife] just told you, not all of my relatives were against the wedding with her because of her being black. But my niece said "Ah, uncle, why are you going to marry a black?" I said to her "Her color is not important to me, it is the type of person that she is, she works hard."

The absence of cross-class solidarity among Euro-Brazilians and the strong interracial intraclass allegiances generate reluctance on the part of many Euro-Brazilians to absolutely reject Afro-Brazilians as romantic or marital partners whom they grew up with as children. In contrast to the United States,

Afro- and Euro-Brazilians in the same socioeconomic position typically live in the same residential communities, socialize, and work together (Telles 1992). Moreover, Afro-Brazilians are not subjected to the white terrorism (being beaten, being murdered, being rejected by white neighbors and co-workers) that is characteristic of the United States (Dollard 1937; Powdermaker 1939; Blee 1991; Segrest 1994). There is a lack of generalized white terrorism and hostility of working-class Euro-Brazilians toward the Afro-Brazilian community. Finally, nonelite Euro-Brazilians in Vasalia are reluctant to self-identify as white and do not usually engage in white supremacist organizing.

Rogerio is a successful thirty-eight-year-old construction worker married to a white woman. As the son of illiterate plantation workers, Rogerio has achieved significant upward mobility. He completed his primary education, purchased a new six-room home, opened a savings account, and acquired membership at the white-controlled Village Club. Rogerio is considered very successful by Vasalian measures. However, his white wife's parents initially opposed her relationship with him. While carefully avoiding the topic of his white in-laws' opposition to his marriage with their daughter, Rogerio provides a dramatic example of how white elite resistance to interracial marriage may occasionally result in violence directed against the black male.

> *Rogerio* If a white man impregnates a black woman, everyone says, "A morena is going to be born!" If a black man impregnates a white woman, they will curse him. There will be a fight. [White relatives] will do everything to humiliate him. This includes killing him. This problem exists. It really exists.
>
> *JW* Murder!
>
> *Rogerio* Yes, murder. I know many examples. I know some cases when the black man impregnated their [white] daughter. Because she was white she had to hide her romance and love making with him. In the end, when they [her relatives] discovered that she was pregnant they wanted to kill [her black lover].

This same incident was also reported by Euro-Brazilians, but they argued that this type of white terrorism is less common than the *informal* pressures that are applied to discourage interracial marriages between the children of white landowners and Afro-Brazilians. While Rogerio described the racism that other Afro-Brazilian men had faced, he *never* mentioned the opposition that he personally encountered when he began to date and subsequently marry his white wife.

In a separate private conversation that I had with Nilani, Rogerio's wife, she described her parents' rejection of Rogerio because of his predominant African ancestry. She said that her father strongly opposed her dating Rogerio and then tried to block her marriage by insisting on what Nilani considered to be an excessively long engagement period. She had decided to not engage in premarital sexual relations with Rogerio although she had been sexually active with her former white boyfriend. This was another motivation for not delaying the marriage. Her father tried to force her to cancel or delay her marriage plans by insisting upon a one-year engagement period. She had to threaten to run away with Rogerio in order to obtain her father's approval for a three-month engagement.

The undesirability of dark-skinned Afro-Brazilians as appropriate romantic partners for Euro-Brazilians is further articulated in the national media. An example is the negative public response to interracial romance in television programs. Black actress ZeZe Motta described the strong opposition by the viewing audience to her television romance with a wealthy white male character:

> Miss Motta, the actress, spoke the other day about the slow pace (of Afro-Brazilian upward mobility) and the difficulties of change. She said that when the powerful TV Globo network finally agreed to have a black female lead in a recent prime-time soap opera, blacks saw this as a success. But opinion polls showed a barrage of angry reactions to the story of a rich [white] young man who fell in love with a black woman, portrayed by Miss Motta. "The racism was much worse than anyone expected," said Miss Motta, adding that the series' white author and the male lead received many hostile phone calls. (Margolis and Carter 1979)

Interracial relationships between social equals are not approved of, and have been rare on Brazilian television. They face strong opposition both in the television land of soap operas and in the town of Vasalia. While a handful of lower-middle-class Euro-Brazilian women had married Afro-Brazilians (typically during an advanced state of pregnancy), none of the elite Euro-

Brazilian women interviewed reported having ever dated an Afro-Brazilian man. They had somehow learned, while being explicitly told that "everyone is equal," not to date or marry Afro-Brazilian men.

Previous researchers have also found that African ancestry is a barrier to interracial marriage, even for light-skinned Afro-Brazilians. Describing race relations in a rural town outside of Salvador, Bahia, in 1952, Harry Hutchinson describes the resistance to a white elite daughter's marriage to an educated black professional:

> In another case a white girl of the local upper class of the town is engaged to a *preto*, who is an engineer in Salvador, but whose family has roots in Vila Reconçavo. There was great resistance to the engagement on the part of the girl's family, and all but her friends felt that, although she had a good "catch," that is, a successful man, he was too dark for her. This in spite of the fact that the girl's father is a *branca da terra* (of mixed ancestry) and that her grandmother was dark skinned. . . . One great bar between the upper class of "aristocratic whites" and those below them is that of marriage. The white of the second class may sometimes be acceptable to the upper class because he is white; but the chances are heavy against the marriage of an "aristocrat" white with an *homen de côr* (Hutchinson 1952, 40–41).[6]

Previous researchers found resistance to mestiçagem among Euro-Brazilians committed to maintaining a genealogy of predominant or exclusive European ancestry. In Vasalia, the Euro-Brazilian elite often uses terms such as "clean blood" when describing their family. Clean blood, that is, *no trace of known or observable African ancestry*, is often cited as a criterion for dating and marriage by elite and middle-class Euro-Vasalians. Despite the Brazilian insistence that "we are all racially mixed," I encountered no members of the Vasalian elite who claimed any African ancestry. In fact, one of the most significant distinctions in the discourses between the elite and nonelite Euro-Vasalians is the insistence of the elite on its racially pure and racially unmixed lineage. If there was evidence of non-European ancestors, the elite defined them as Indians, never as mulattos or Afro-Brazilians. African ancestors were thus conveniently converted into Indians or simply "erased" from the family records. While Vasalians were able to identify whites of poor origins who had married white members of the middle or upper middle class, Vasalians had difficulty identifying a single Afro-Brazilian of any class who had married into the elite.

Middle-class Euro-Brazilians used a binary classification system that places light- and dark-skinned Afro-Brazilians squarely in the same racial box in terms of their undesirability as marital partners. This contradicts the belief held by the light-skinned Afro-Brazilians (who typically describe themselves as morenos or pardos rather than negros or pretos) that they constitute an intermediate category from their darker-skinned Afro-Brazilian peers. For the elites, these distinctions were not relevant (see Scheper-Hughes 1992).

Raquel, a thirty-one-year-old great-great granddaughter of Italian and Portuguese plantation owners, is married to Dr. Giovanni, a successful physician in Vasalia. She describes how her mother had raised her to treat all Vasalians as equal. When she began to consider the issue of interracial marriage, the discussion shifts to an analysis of her mother's belief that Afro-Brazilians are not desirable or suitable marriage partners for middle-class whites.

> In my family, my mother always tried to put questions of [racial inequality] very natural, right. Thinking [about race] from the religious point of view, all are equal, no one is superior to anyone else. But I believe that, in spite of this, despite not admitting that [she believed whites are superior]. This "everyone is equal" and not wanting to pass on [racial] prejudice to us. I believe that this was meant at the level of friendship, of treating people well at work—in professional life. But I don't know if she would continue to believe in this equality if I had suddenly married a black person and she had [mixed-race] grandchildren. I believe that in spite of not admitting to being racist she would not be pleased with an interracial marriage.

At another point during the interview, Raquel described a shift in her consciousness that occurred when her white husband asked her if she had ever considered marriage with a black man. Raquel revealed that it was not until she thought about being the *mother of a black child* that she recognized that she had racist attitudes.

> I never used to stop to consider the questions "Could I marry a black person?" "How would it be if I had a black child?" Really, because

I have never been attracted to black men. Then and until that difficult question (would I have considered marrying a black man) and
my responding yes—suddenly, the question that [my husband] asked,
"Could you have married a black man?" made me aware [of my
racism]. Then I really knew that I never felt attracted to a person of
the black race. It was the only moment [that I was confronted with
my racism]. We never discussed this because we behave normally
(in an nonracist manner) in front of blacks. The question [of our rac-
ism] was always a question that we never asked.

The *naturalness* of Raquel's exclusive attraction (and that of Afro-
Brazilian women) to white men is rarely, if ever questioned in Vasalia. This
preference is seen as logical. The desire for white or lighter children, while
having polite professional relationships or friendships with Afro-Brazilians,
is not something that Raquel had ever considered in the context of racism.
She had never considered her desire for white men as a reflection of racist
attitudes. This is partially due to the emphasis Vasalians place upon the absolute and overt rejection of Afro-Brazilians when defining racism. They typically don't consider more covert forms of racism such as *not* considering
blacks or dark-skinned Afro-Brazilians as suitable marital partners.

Class divisions and social segregation between elites and nonelites have
not generated cross-class solidarity among Euro-Brazilians. Thus, Euro-
Brazilians elites typically live class-segregated lives and rarely, if ever, seri-
ously consider marriage or close friendships with individuals outside of their
class position. In most cases, nonelites are considered undesirable candidates
for marriage. However, in a context where abortion is criminalized and where
Vasalians often engage in unprotected premarital sex, premarital pregnancies
can occasionally lead to marriage across class between Euro-Brazilians.

These class divisions are also partially responsible for interracial class
allegiances among working-class Afro- and Euro-Brazilians. It is important
to note that interracial relationships do occur *outside* of marriage between
white elites and women of color. However, these relationships do not threaten
white supremacy. North American scholars of racial caste systems have argued that sexual relations between white men and African American women
is a consequence of racism, not an antiracist act (Dollard 1937; Powdermaker
1939).

Afro-Brazilians recognize that their marriages to nonelite Euro-Brazilians are sometimes motivated by the desire for class mobility. I was told of several cases involving financially successful Afro-Brazilian men and white women from less-privileged background. These marriages often faced opposition by the white parents. Carmen, a thirty-year-old unmarried light-skinned Afro-Brazilian who works as a domestic servant for a white middle-class family, illustrates this point. "He is more or less black. . . . But he is very rich. Very rich. They call him Pelé.[7] He is the owner of the funeral home. . . . Her father, the [white] father of the girl that married him, was against the marriage because she is a white with blue eyes. Then the father didn't want the wedding to take place, but she just consented because he is so wealthy. She just recently got married and lives very well now."

Class mobility, although sometimes a motivation for poor whites to marry interracially, is not always a sufficient incentive for poor Vasalians of multiracial ancestry to marry Afro-Brazilians. For example, Shayla,[8] a sixty-five-year-old poor Afro-Brazilian women of mixed Portuguese and African ancestry, described her poor mother's opposition to her even dating a black pharmacist when she was a young woman. Although this man had had a lucrative business by rural standards, he was still unacceptable to her mother, a poor white woman.

Shayla He listened to my breathing . . . and then he gave me a cough medicine. But then, I overused the medicine. I drank all of it from one day to the next. It ended my cough suddenly, but it made my throat itch so much that I almost died. So when he saw me again, he asked me, "So how about your cough?" . . . He had a mouth filled with pure gold. Sometimes I used to watch him like this and I used to say "This is a pharmacist." I thought he was very handsome.

FWT Would your mother have allowed you to marry this man?

Shayla Would she allow this? My mother was very proud. If I was willing to look at him from a distance, to observe him, I had to do it out of anyone's sight.

Husband But [her mother] would not allow it because he was black.

Shayla That's right. Because my mother is the daughter of a Portuguese woman [and a mulatto]. It is her in that picture [pointing to a framed portrait of her mother hanging on the wall].

Husband My wife was young then. The pharmacist in the town was very
    dark skinned. She thought he was handsome, but her mother did not
    allow her to date him because he was black.

Shayla's mother's attitude illustrates how even impoverished women of
salient African ancestry may strongly oppose their children even *dating* a
successful Afro-Brazilian despite their material interests. It also reveals the
degree of antiblack racism that can be found in multiracial families that include Afro-Brazilian family members. Escape from poverty is not necessar-
ily a sufficient inducement in Brazil to compensate for the African ancestry
of Afro-Brazilians when poor families make a decision about the selection
of desirable marital or dating partners.

    Another example of opposition to "mixed" marriage involves Mani, a
dark-skinned Afro-Brazilian woman and her husband, a light-skinned Afro-
Brazilian man of multiracial heritage. Mani is a twenty-seven-year-old woman
who describes herself as preta. She married her light-skinned husband, a mulatto, at the age of seventeen.

    While I was viewing Mani's wedding photos, I began to suspect that
her husbands' parents had not attended her wedding because they did not appear in any of the photos in her wedding album. When I asked if her in-laws
had attended her wedding ceremony, she reluctantly told me that they had
opposed their son dating her because they wanted him to marry his white
girlfriend. When her husband decided to marry her and not his white girlfriend, his German-Brazilian father and his Afro-Brazilian mother opposed
the marriage and refused to attend the ceremony.

    Mani denied that her in-laws were racists and that their rejection of her
was at all related to her dark skin color. Although she continued to repeat
that there was no evidence that her in-laws' preference for her husband's white
girlfriend was racially based, her *white* female friend directly challenged her
and argued that her dark skin color and African appearance was the primary
reason that her in-laws opposed her marriage to their son. Mani's case further illustrates the concerns that Ariana and Tatiana expressed regarding the
power differential that can occur in marriages between lighter and darker partners. Although Mani's husband is not white (he is described as a mulatto,
but self-identifies as moreno), he appears to humiliate her by openly conducting an affair with his former girlfriend, now his mistress. She has pro-

duced a white daughter for him while Mani has produced a son, who she refers to as a "black." She expressed feelings of profound depression and feels that she has no hope of improving her life.

A final example of how opposition to mestiçagem operates among the white working classes involves Allesandro, who is from a very poor family of Italian origins. His family, a fourth-generation Italian-Brazilian family, was described to me by Ariana as one who "adores brown-skinned people." Ariana described to me the response of some of his white family members to his marriage to a light-skinned mulatta.

> *Ariana* He suffered a lot of obstacles because he married her [Afro-Brazilian wife], Alex's wife of the pharmacy. He and his family suf-fered a lot of [social] barriers. He is one of the [white men] families that loves dark-skinned people, they adore dark-skinned people. The grandmother, however, is horrified by blacks, can't even look at them.
>
> *FWT* So he had a lot of problems?
>
> *Ariana* Yes. He did. One of his brothers, the one I said that doesn't come to visit because he married a brown-skinned woman. His brother nearly never comes here. But [his wife] isn't black, she is your color (pointing to my color). I am speaking the truth.

This is another example of a muted critique of the racial democracy. While not all white members of Allesandro's natal family rejected him, he was so-cially ostracized by his brother and grandmother in response to his marriage to a mulatta.

Conclusion

Latin American scholars have described the valorization of whiteness and the movements away from blackness among dark-skinned Afro–Latin Americans. In this chapter I have argued that this practice of embranqueci-mento is not simply a policy imposed by the elites but a practice embraced by working-class Afro-Brazilians.[9] The white supremacist aesthetic hierar-chies that I found operating among Afro-Brazilians in Vasalia operate against the formation of a black-identified antiracist middle-class community.

In a context in which the most educated and economically privileged Afro-Brazilians usually attempt to reproduce a family that is both socially and biologically whiter, they typically transfer their material and social resources to lighter (ideally white) children and partners. These movements toward whiteness illustrate how Afro-Brazilians engage in practices that generate distance between themselves and dark-skinned Afro-Brazilians. Furthermore, the reproduction of a whiter family in biological and cultural terms reinforces the semiotic link between blackness and poverty while also failing to generate an alternative aesthetic hierarchy for dark-skinned Afro-Brazilian children. Consequently, it is virtually impossible for Afro-Brazilians to produce an educated self-identified black middle class to emerge as a collective political entity in Vasalia. Thus, there is an absence of a critical mass of Afro-Brazilians in Vasalia who are motivated to generate an antiracist symbolic and material order.

This phenomenon of upward mobility being accompanied by whitening has been documented in other parts of Afro–Latin America. As the British anthropologist Peter Wade notes in his study of blackness and race mixture in Colombia, "If upwardly mobile blacks marry lighter-skinned people, blackness is inevitably bleached out of the middle strata of society, maintaining the overall correlation between black and poor. And this correlation will remain as long as black upward mobility and its acceptance remain individualistic and conditional" (1993, 297).

I found contradictions and tensions between the public discourse of mestiçagem and the private opposition to marriage with dark-skinned Afro-Brazilians among both Afro- and Euro-Brazilians in Vasalia. I documented the struggles that Vasalians encounter as they manage the gap between the desires of Afro-Brazilians committed to *embranquecimento* and of those Vasalians committed to maintaining a genealogy exclusively of European ancestry. While an ideology of embranquecimento encourages and rewards Afro-Brazilians for producing lighter children, Euro-Brazilians often resist and oppose this mestiçagem.

The only effective resistance to mestiçagem that I found in Vasalia was among Euro-Brazilians motivated by antiblack racism. I documented several forms of resistance that included Euro-Brazilians pressuring their family members to reject blacks as marriage partners, murdering black men who had impregnated white women, and social ostracism of white men married to Afro-Brazilian women.

This orientation toward whitening ones' children reproduces a symbolic order that links whiteness to material privilege while linking blackness to impoverishment and inferiority. Thus, those physical traits that signify European ancestry remain symbolically linked with material privilege and status. Whitening practices that reproduce the symbolic and material link between light skin and social mobility do not challenge white supremacist ideologies and serve to teach dark-skinned Afro-Brazilian (and Euro-Brazilian) children that the most effective way of improving their situation and that of their children is to whiten them by reproducing a family with a lighter partner of European ancestry.

CHAPTER 6

Memory: White Inflation and WillfulForgetting

*Whatever is unnamed, undepicted in images, whatever is omitted from biography,
censored in collections of letters, whatever is buried in the memory by the collapse of
meaning . . . this will become, not merely unspoken, but unspeakable.*
—Adrienne Rich (1979, 199)

*Indeed, much of the cultural debate in Brazil since the 1985 transition has
reinforced the government position that only "forgetting" the past can insure a
peaceful democratic future.*
—Joan Dassin (1989, 115)

*Another aspect of the Latin American ideal of whitening has been the attempt to cover up
all traces of the black presence following abolition.*
—Carlos Hasenbalg (1996, 165)

On 14 December 1890, Rui Barbosa,
the Brazilian minister of finance, ordered that the federal archives of slave
registration books be burned (Toplin 1971, 235). It is significant that one of
the first acts of the Nova Republica (New Republic) during the transition period after slavery was abolished was an act of "willful forgetting," or destroying records that testified to Brazil's long history of African slavery. This
practice of whitening records is also engaged in by Vasalians in private and
public spheres. In this chapter I examine memorializing practices that
Vasalians use to dis-remember slaves and maximize the distance between
Vasalians and African-descent Brazilians.

National memory is an arena of struggle for the *movimento negro* and
other antiracist activists in Brazil (Hanchard 1994; Winant 1994; Warren
1997). Less theoretical attention, however, has been given to the memories

and memorializing practices of families and local communities in analyses of racism and antiracism in Brazil. How do memorializing practices of ordinary Brazilians sustain white supremacy? What is actively dis-remembered? It is the everyday practices of remembering and forgetting that are of concern to me in this chapter.

This chapter is divided into three sections. I begin with a discussion of white inflation in the federal census records. I examine the practice of embranquecimento as it occurs in the registration practices of Afro-Brazilians and connect this to an artificial inflation in the number of officially (nationally) recognized whites in federal census records. I then move to a discussion of narrative practices that minimize and erase Africans and Afro-Brazilians in Vasalia. In the third and final section I analyze the family photo albums of a working-class Afro-Brazilian family and a middle-class Euro-Brazilian family to explore how this practice of dis-remembering African-descent ancestors whitens family genealogies in Vasalia.

White Inflation in Federal Records

Various scholars have commented upon the unreliability and difficulty interpreting the meaning of Brazilian statistics on color/race.[1] The undercounting and invisibility of the black Brazilian population was identified as a serious national problem by a nongovernmental organization (NGO), the Brazilian Institute of Social and Economic Analysis (IBASE) in 1991. In response, IBASE and several other organizations initiated a media campaign to discourage the practice of whitening (white inflation on census records) by nonwhites on the 1991 census.[2] Television commercials, radio announcements, posters, pamphlets, forums, and workshops were held that urged African-descent Brazilians: "*Não deixe sua cor passar em branco: responda com bom censo*" (Don't let your color pass [or be covered] by whiteness).

Regina Domingues, an Afro-Brazilian staff researcher at IBASE and coordinator of a campaign to increase Afro-Brazilian visibility in governmental records, comments on how this absence of data supports the invisibility of Afro-Brazilians and the racism they encounter.

> The myth of racial democracy has combined with public policy to lead Brazilians to believe that there is equal opportunity for all and

no racial conflict here. During eras of dictatorship, discussing the racial question meant risking your life, and the subject of racism became securely taboo. The desire to whiten Brazil resulted in removals of queries about color from the census forms of 1900, 1920, and 1970. The consequences of this attitude go far beyond the simple lack of census data which could have enriched research on the black population. The most serious result is that populations of color, in addition to losing their identity, have been turned socially and politically invisible. Once they no longer officially existed, no policies attending to their needs were necessary. (Domingues 1988)

More than a decade before this campaign was initiated, Abdias do Nascimento,[3] the first black Brazilian elected to the Brazilian National Congress, speaks of this problem: "Lighter mulattos (and even some who are not so light) describe themselves as whites. Blacks often identify themselves as mulatto, or mestiço or pardo or some other euphemism" ([1979] 1989, 78). Nascimento, who considers this a consequence of racism, explains how this practice can be interpreted as nonracist within the context of the Brazilian racial democracy. "Since 1950 race and color data have been omitted from the census information in Brazil on the assumption that an act of 'white magic' can eliminate ethnicity by decree. This process occurs under the rationale that it is founded on the precept of social justice that everyone is Brazilian. . . . The reality of race relations is masked and any information that blacks could use in their struggle for social justice is withheld" (ibid., 80).

The national ideology of embranquecimento is practiced at the local level by Afro-Brazilians who lighten themselves when they self-identify on official records such as birth, marriage, and census forms despite how they are recognized and treated socially in everyday life. In Brazil, a "one-drop rule," which is the inverse of the U.S. rule,[4] enables any Brazilian with any degree of European or indigenous ancestry to claim a nonblack identity. This allows virtually all African-descent Brazilians to avoid black identification on official documents. Thus, blacks, like Indians in the nineteenth-century U.S., were described by Vasalians as a "vanishing" race, one that is being absorbed into the Brazilian national population.

White Inflation: Federal and Local Records

I use the term white inflation to refer to a phenomenon that is not unique to Brazil and has been documented in other Latin American countries. Anthropologists working in the Caribbean and Latin America have noted that African-descent people with white ancestors routinely lighten themselves on official documents by claiming a white or brown identity, despite how they are counteridentified by others in their community (Hurston 1990 [1938]; Scheper-Hughes 1992). In Vasalia, children are not required to accompany their parents to the registrar's office when their births are officially recorded. Until recently, many children in Vasalia were not born in a hospital, so their birth was typically registered by one of their parents weeks, months, or even years later. It is at this moment that Afro-Brazilian children can enter the official records as "whites."

When I examined the birth certificates of Afro-Brazilians in Vasalia—individuals referred to as mulattos, morenos, or negros—I found that approximately one-third had been registered by their parents as brancos on their federal birth certificates. The other two-thirds were registered as pardos, a category that hides more than it reveals since, until 1991, this category included indigenous/Brazilian Indians and a mixed-race person of any degree of African, European, and/or indigenous ancestry.

In private conversations, Afro-Brazilians often confessed to me that they had registered their children as brancos, even though they recognized their children are morenos or mulattos of African ancestry.[5] Aside from artificially inflating the number of legal whites in the official population, this also generates a discrepancy between the *social* color and the *official* color of Afro-Brazilians. Henrique, the Afro-Brazilian father of a daughter who he described as a mulatta but whom he registered as a branca, describes this practice: "Because, for example, when you go to register an infant at the office of vital records, the infant does not have to accompany you. Therefore, sometimes an infant is really black, but you can [register] her as white. A man will say that his child is white and [the official] is going to write down that the child is white. But we know the color that we really are."

This action compromises census data and other official records because there is no correspondence between how individuals are socially constructed and treated in the local racial hierarchy and their registered identity (legal construction) in birth, death, and marital documents. In Vasalia, the Afro-Brazilians who told me that they were registered as brancos on official documents expressed pride in having this whiter identity on official forms. I found that as long as light-skinned Afro-Brazilians do not claim the social privileges of being treated as white in everyday interactions, their registered white identity is not usually challenged. A similar practice was described by the U.S. black folklorist Zora Neale Hurston in the 1930s during her field research in Jamaica.

> [It] is so arranged in Jamaica that a person may be black by birth but white by proclamation. That is, he gets himself declared legally white. . . . The joke about being white on the census records and colored otherwise has its curious angles. The English seem to feel that "If it makes a few of you happy and better colonials to be officially white, very well. You are white on the census rolls." The Englishman keeps on being very polite and cordial to the legal whites in public, but ignores them utterly in private and social life. And the darker Negroes do not forget how they came to be white. ([1938] 1990, 8)

Hurston's description of 1930s Jamaica paralleled what I found in Vasalia. Registered "whites" of salient African ancestry in Vasalia are not challenged in public. The elite appear to have little interest in what their "official" or legal color is since they carry the sign of their ancestry on their bodies and will be treated accordingly by them.

Local Memory: The Erasure of Afro-Brazilians and Slavery from Local Histories

Despite Vasalia's long history of plantation slavery, many of the Afro-Brazilians I spoke with denied that it had ever operated there. This is particularly surprising, given the fact that Vasalia is located in a region that had one of the highest concentration of slaves in Brazil when slavery was abolished in 1888. Thomas Skidmore notes: "By the time the abolitionist campaign began, the national slave population was concentrated—from the standpoint of absolute numbers—in the three major coffee-growing provinces of São Paulo, Minas Gerais, and Rio de Janeiro" ([1974] 1993, 43).

Despite the dependence of the local coffee plantation economy on slave labor, African-origin and Afro-Brazilian slaves have been all but erased from local histories and from community narratives. On 13 May 1992, residents of Vasalia chose not to commemorate the abolition of slavery and to just "forget it," while less than seven hours away in the city of Rio de Janeiro, there were parades and speeches on that day in recognition of abolition. When I asked a middle-aged Afro-Brazilian woman why there was no recognition of this federal holiday in Vasalia, she looked at me with irritation and replied "That [slavery] happened in the past, it is not important today."

This type of active forgetting and refusal to retain any memories of slavery has been documented by anthropologists working in rural areas with significant African-descent populations in the Northeast (Harris 1952; Scheper-Hughes 1992). Less published data exist on the retention of memories of Africans and slavery in the Southeast. Marvin Harris interpreted this lack of memory to the individuals' possible status as descendants of runaway slaves. However, this may be only a partial explanation since it is cannot be assumed that everyone who fails to remember the history of slavery is descended from runaway slaves. Writing of a town in the northeastern state of Bahia, Harris offers the following interpretation of the failure to remember slavery: "The oldest resident of Baixa de Gamba, who claims to be ninety, insists that no one in his family nor in the community was ever a slave. . . . The failure to retain any memories of slavery suggests that his ancestry may perhaps have been members of *quilombos* (communities of freed slaves). Few persons in this rural group are aware of an African heritage, and the bondage of their ancestors is known to them only second-hand from persons who learned something about the history of Negro slavery in school" (1952, 50). An alternative interpretation is that this resident is engaged in a willful "act of forgetting," a strategy for maintaining a sense of dignity by distancing himself from the degradation of slavery.

Local Memories

The history of local slavery in Vasalia, like racism, is a taboo subject in public discussions. During my period of residence, no one ever mentioned local slavery to me and interviews with current students and teachers confirmed that the history of local slavery is not taught in elementary school in

Vasalia. Direct observation of classroom teaching, private conversations, and public discussions suggested that only the *abolition* of slavery is included in the history lessons in primary school. Interviews with residents of Vasalia revealed that the only thing they remembered having learned from teachers and textbooks about racism in Brazil was that racism ended when Princess Isabella liberated the African slaves by signing the Golden Law of Abolition in 1888. Few Vasalians knew much about the actual experience of slavery and the conditions under which slaves had lived.

Carla invited me and my research partner Jonathan to visit her at the Catholic primary school where she and her sister Catarina taught. Carla is the twenty-one-year-old great-granddaughter of African-born slaves and refers to herself as a morena. She never mentions that she is the descendant of African slaves nor does she describe herself as linked in any way to a history of slavery. During my visit I listened to her present a lecture on quilombos. The lecture began with Carla drawing two hands, one brown, the other white. These two hands were embraced in a handshake. Carla talked about Brazilian racial harmony before giving a brief lecture on free blacks who had escaped from slavery and formed quilombos.

In her lecture on slavery in Brazil, Carla did not describe the actual conditions of slavery. The lecture (like the school textbook) focused on quilombos and not on the realities that the vast majority of slaves endured. In Carla's narrative, slavery was not a national institution but was contained in the northeastern region of Brazil. She discussed slavery as if it had no relationship to her or any of the children in her classroom.

Carla presented no information to her students that suggested or revealed that slavery had existed in the region of Vasalia. Students were *not* told that the founding families in this community had established their plantations with the slave labor of African and Indians. As I listened to this lecture I could think only about the fact that this schoolhouse was located on a former plantation that had operated with slave labor. According to Carla, "Slavery occurred a long time ago" and had no impact on Vasalia. Carla later told me that this was the only lecture of the entire school year devoted to the history of slavery in Brazil.

When asked whether slavery had existed in the local community, Carla replied, "If it did that was a long time ago." Like the majority of Afro-Brazilian residents interviewed, Carla denied any knowledge of her African ancestry, although her father reported that he is the *grandson* of African-born slaves. Her father also reported that he did not discuss the history of slavery with his children, but the physical appearance of the entire family left no doubt that they were of at least a large degree of African ancestry.

Few Vasalians said they had any knowledge about the history of local slavery. Both Afro- and Euro-Brazilians claimed that they did not know that African and Indian slave labor had been used in this region and they had no knowledge that *senzalas* (long narrow shacks where slaves lived) had existed there. Vittorio, a fifty-two-year-old Italian-Brazilian poet and retired police officer, said, "I don't remember if there was slavery here. I don't remember. My parents didn't talk about this. Now [slavery] occurred in places far away, right? . . . But no I think that in our region, if slavery existed, it was minimal. When I was born slavery didn't exist anymore [in Brazil]."

Vittorio's comments were typical of working-class Vasalians. They attempt to deny, forget, or minimize the significance of slavery in the local community while acknowledging that it *had* existed in the past because they knew local residents who were the children of slaves. Many individuals began by saying that "I don't know anything about slavery," only to later reveal that they knew that they were not far removed from it. Three-fourths of the Vasalians I interviewed were two or three generations removed from slavery as the direct descendants of slaves, slave owners, or slave supervisors (overseers). In interviews I conducted with dark-skinned Afro-Brazilians, a typical response to questions about local slavery follows:

FWT Were there slaves in this region?

Tônica I don't know.

FWT You didn't learn about this in school?

Tônica I didn't learn about this. I never attempted to find out if there were any slaves or Indians in this region. I don't think anyone here really knows about this. Would anyone know? The old people here must know [about slavery], right? But I don't know about slavery.

FWT Then no one spoke about this?

Tônica No one spoke of [slavery]. They only talk about the history of Vasalia, how it acquired its name.

Working in the city of Rio de Janeiro in a *morro* (poor community in the hills), white anthropologist Robin Sheriff found a similar pattern of Afro-

Brazilians consciously choosing to forget about slavery and racism. Based on in-depth interviews with urban Afro-Brazilians, Sheriff argues that "very few informants in fact, were able to recall hearing stories about the slavery era, although the grandparents and great grandparents of a number of the older people I knew had in fact, been slaves."[6]

Five of the Afro-Brazilians I interviewed had family members who had offered them oral accounts of slavery as former slaves or as the children of slaves. The Afro-Brazilians reported that they didn't listen to these stories and did not recount them to their children. The period of slavery was dismissed as irrelevant to their life today, although many lived in social and material conditions only slightly better than their slave ancestors.

Anthropologists conducting research in the Northeast region of Brazil have also found this failure of African-descent Brazilians to link their current status of impoverishment to racism and their history as the descendants of slaves. Describing the self-identification of African-descent residents of a northeastern shanty town, Nancy Scheper-Hughes writes:

> These people are the descendants of a slave and runaway slave-Indian (*caboclo*) population. Yet they do not think to link their current difficulties to a history of slavery and race exploitation. Racism is a disallowed and submerged discourse in Northeast Brazil, so that every bit as much as Wolf's (1982) European peasants, these are a people "without a history." They call themselves simply *os pobres* [the poor] and they describe themselves as *moreno* (brown), almost never as *preto* or *negro* (black). They are "brown," then, as *all* Brazilians, rich and poor, are said to be "brown." In this way, the ideology of "racial democracy," as pernicious as the American ideology of "equality of opportunity," goes unchallenged, uncontested, into another generation. (1992, 90)

My research revealed that contradictions existed between what individuals reported initially that they remembered about their family history and what they willfully forget. Several interviews with dark-skinned Afro-Brazilians suggest that they *chose not to retain memories* of African slave ancestors but that they had some limited knowledge about their African and slave origins.

Tônica, the daughter of a man born into slavery, first denied any knowledge of slavery, then later revealed that her father had been a slave as a child and that she had refused to listen to his recollections of slavery. This refusal to attend to her father's stories, and more importantly, to accounts about the conditions under which slaves lived, means that many Afro-Brazilians do not acknowledge or learn to recognize the continuity between the condition of black slaves and the current material conditions of the majority of poor black Brazilians as underpaid domestic servants and agricultural workers.

Community Memories: Forgetting about Jim Crow-like Racial Segregation

Like local slavery, racial segregation of public spaces was also a taboo subject. During my residence in Vasalia, I never heard anyone talk publicly about segregation of the main streets by color/race. Thus, I was surprised when several Afro-Brazilian men privately discussed this in detail. When asked, "Can you provide any specific examples of racism?" several of them told of Jim Crow–like segregation of the main street, stores, public sidewalks, social clubs, dances, and beauty contests that was a fact of life as recently as 1985. This was not publicly discussed, and most Vasalians would say privately, "That happened a long time ago." White informants confirmed in private, taped interviews that this public segregation by skin color and race had occurred during their lifetimes. More than one-fourth of the interviewees over the age of twenty-five years volunteered this information in interviews. When asked if she had any memories of racism, a dark-skinned self-identified mulatta said:

> *Luisa* No. I cannot remember [any examples of racism in Vasalia].
> *JW* You don't remember any examples? Do you have any memories of segregated social clubs having existed here because some other residents said that there used to be racially segregated clubs?
> *Luisa* Ah! This is true. But a long time has already passed since this happened. There used to be social clubs for brown-skinned people and separate clubs for whites. The Club for Whites was called the Club of Thirteen. You are very well informed (nervous laughter). But this was a long time ago, in the period when I was seventeen or eighteen years old (around 1966).

Prior to this interview, male relatives of this woman had volunteered

this information in an interview when relating how much things had pro-
gressed and changed in Vasalia since their youth. Several white males had
also confirmed that this racially exclusive, whites-only social club had existed and had been organized by an Italian-Brazilian doctor, who had recently
lost his bid to be the first elected mayor of the town. A long time ago for
Luisa turned out to be approximately twenty-eight years before, while other
informants said the end of the racial segregation of the social club and main
street had occurred seven years before (1985). The important point is that
public segregation of the social clubs and the main street ended during the
lifetime of residents over the ages of seven to ten. This would place Jim Crow–
like segregation in the living memories of a significant portion of the local
population.[7]

Using excerpts from the same interview with Luisa, we can see how
she either refused to speak of or had not retained any memories of racial segregation of the main street or stores. She denied having ever experienced this,
although as she was forty-six years old, she would have encountered it as a
young woman.

JW Do you have any memory of these [segregated sidewalks]?
Luisa No. I did not know that this existed there [Boa Vista]?
JW Ah!
Luisa How many years ago did this occur?
JW Some people have said "many" years ago and others have said that
    it ended seven years ago.
Luisa Look. I studied in Boa Vista for twenty-three years and I don't
    remember this.

Unlike the segregation of private social clubs, racial segregation of public sidewalks is not subtle or covert. It would have been impossible for a poor
and dark-skinned black Brazilian to have avoided it since there is only one
main street in Boa Vista. Moreover, several in Luisa's age cohort, family members and colleagues, recalled that this type of segregation had existed, although
they minimized it and distanced themselves from the practice. Other informants, while acknowledging that this type of racial segregation had been practiced *during their lifetimes*, framed it as "minor" and something that occurred
a long time ago.

This active forgetting of racial segregation, combined with the absence of public documentation in schoolbooks of this form of racism, is one barrier to public recognition that overt racial discrimination existed in the past. It is also another way that Brazilians minimize and deny the racial animosity that existed and another way to espouse the racial democracy myth. Although not codified in law, racial segregation was both routine and publicly enforced in Boa Vista and its satellite town, Vasalia. This use of memory and forgetting, particularly among blacks, mulattos, and poor whites who constitute the numerical majority, sustains the myth that racism is not today and has not been a problem since the abolition of slavery

Whitening Narratives

Mixed-race Afro-Brazilians typically avoid naming their black ancestors when reciting the oral history of their families. The Afro-Brazilians interviewed did not pass on memories of the experiences of their own African-descent family members. This was in striking contrast to the descriptions that they willingly provided of their European ancestors (generally plantation owners) and mixed-race ancestors. Most refused to discuss the topic with me and considered it rude for me to inquire about their non-European forebears. Although life history interviews revealed that most of my mixed-race informants were only two or three generations removed from slavery, they typically could not provide even the first name of their African ancestors two generations removed.

Returning to the work of Zora Neale Hurston in Jamaica, we see another example of this construction of genealogies in ways that erase black ancestors while providing linkages to Europeans and to whiteness. Hurston notes:

> When a Jamaican is born of a black woman and some English or
> Scotsman, the black mother is literally and figuratively kept out of
> sight as far as possible, but no one is allowed to forget that white
> father, however, questionable the circumstances of birth. You hear
> about "My father this and my father that, and my father who was
> English, you know," until you get the impression that he or she *had*
> no mother. Black skin is so utterly condemned that the black mother
> is not going to be mentioned or exhibited. You get the impression

that these virile Englishmen do not require women for reproduction. ([1938] 1990, 8)

In Vasalia, the repeated omissions of the names of African and African-descent relatives and the repetitive naming of one's European ancestors and relatives occurred whenever someone was introduced to me or my white partner. During our first three months, whenever Jonathan was introduced to anyone, they would invariably compare his white skin, straight black hair, and hazel eyes to one of their family members as far back as four generations while never mentioning a single African or Afro-Brazilian ancestor.

In Vasalia, prestige is directly related to how much distance one can put between oneself and Africans in terms of physical appearance, cultural traits, and economic status. This distancing is accomplished by not allowing oneself to reflect upon the lives of African ancestors who had been exploited as slave laborers. There was a high degree of shame attached to being descendants of slaves, so in private interviews when asked about their ancestors, dark-skinned Afro-Brazilians came close to tears and were unable to utter the word African when asked about their heritage. In one case, when a very dark-skinned woman of African ancestry replied, "I don't know who my ancestors are," her white husband interrupted, and, while describing his wife as *escura* (dark), told her that she was of African ancestry.

The management of individual and collective memories of Afro-Brazilian ancestors is linked to the management of racism by Afro- and Euro-Brazilians. Memories of African slaves ancestors have been an important means for African Americans to establish an antiracist identity in the United States. It has also been a way to directly challenge white supremacy and Anglo hegemony. This collective memory is one of the ways that a national U.S. black community has been established and continues to reproduce itself from generation to generation (Gwaltney 1980).

An example of the important role that memory plays in the reproduction of antiracist identities can be found in the work of U.S. black anthropologist John Langston Gwaltney. In his book *Drylongso: A Self-Portrait of Black America*, there is a section entitled "The Legacy of Slavery," in which black Americans discuss their relationship to slavery and the stories that were passed down in their families. One of his informants, a thirty-something man born in Georgia, describes himself in relation to his slave ancestors. "In many

FIGURE 17. Edimar, his wife, Madalena, and their son Glauber. Edimar, the son of Dona Rosaria, was the first black man in Vasalia to secure a membership in the white country club ten years ago. *(Photo by the author.)*

ways I was more of a slave than most of my black ancestors. At least they knew they were slaves, and it was only their physical bodies and actions that their enemies could control" (1980, 39). Unlike this African American quoted by Gwaltney, none of the Afro-Brazilians interviewed described themselves as linked in any way to slaves when asked to describe their origins. If pushed, some of the men acknowledged that they had some slave ancestors, but this was done with much shame and reluctance. The majority said either that they had no African ancestors or that they had no knowledge of their origins and thus were probably not of African descent.

Joaquim, a sixty-five-year-old dark-skinned Afro-Brazilian and the grandson of slaves from a poor family of coffee plantation workers, describes why his black father never discussed slavery and never passed on any stories or remembrances of his life to his children. "His job was working and taking care of life—he didn't like to talk of the past. The past, sometimes it wasn't very good, right? There were things that happened that it's not worth it to discuss. Can you understand this? Because sometimes the past was terrible, then you leave [memories] of it behind? This [slavery] was awful. Then you leave the [memory of slavery] because you don't want to continue remembering that later, right?"[8] What is it that must be forgotten? For Joaquim, it is the brutality of slavery, a practice that is not consistent with Brazil's image of itself as a place of relative racial harmony both during and after slavery.

Discussions of the horrors of slavery are carefully avoided in Vasalia. I heard few oral accounts of the conditions that slaves endured. Stanley Stein provides us with a portrait of the mundane and violent barbarism to which slaves were routinely subjected by their white owners in this same region. His description of the conditions of slavery is what remains unspeakable in Vasalia.

> Most visible symbol of the master's authority over the slave, the whip. . . . An ingenious, labor-saving variation of the whip was re-ported by ex-slaves. This was a water-driven "codfish" by which a whip secured to a revolving water-wheel lashed slaves tied to a bench. So widespread was use of the lash. . . . Only slightly less brutal than the whippings were the hours spent by male and female slaves alike in the *tronco*, a form of heavy iron stock common on plantations. Arms and legs were imprisoned together forcing the victim to sit hunched forward with arms next to the ankles, or to lie on one side. This was the *tronco duplo*; the *tronco simples* merely imprisoned legs.[9]

What Stein describes is what must be forgotten in order for Brazilian slavery to be described today as fairly benign. Joaquim, like other Afro-Brazilians interviewed, reported that he never passed on any stories of his grandfather, an African-born slave, to his children. Interviews with five of his children confirmed that he had never discussed with them the history of slavery or of his maternal grandparents' experiences as slaves. Several of his daughters vehemently denied being the descendants of slaves, despite hav-ing been asked to represent African countries such as Angola in the city pa-rade. Joaquim constantly mentioned his Portuguese ancestors (slaveowners) and his sister, who had green eyes and light hair. His grandmother had es-sentially been taken as the concubine of a Portuguese slaveowner and sexu-ally exploited.

In conversations and discussions with four of Joaquim's children rang-ing in age from nineteen to forty-six, none voluntarily acknowledged any connection to slaves. In fact, his two youngest daughters, Carla and Catarina, denied having any African lineage although Carla had not been allowed to compete or participate in the local beauty contest for brancas and had to compete in the morena beauty contest for African-descent women. In private conversations, she expressed contempt for dark-skinned Afro-Brazilians and had no close friendships with any Afro-Brazilians. She carefully avoided dating and socializing with Brazilians of African ancestry. All of her closest friends were Luso- and Italian-Brazilians.

During an in-depth life history interview, Henrique, the forty-three-year-old son of Joaquim, also initially denied any knowledge of his African ancestry. He later confessed that one of his great grandparents was an African slave and the other a Portuguese slaveowner. Another Afro-Brazilian informant, Tônica, the *daughter* of a former slave, was also reluctant to acknowledge that she was of any African ancestry when questioned about her heritage. Tônica describes herself as escura and is described as a preta by nonfamily members. Her appearance places her squarely in the black category in Vasalia. Her poor white husband described her as escura, which is the polite term used for a very dark-skinned Afro-Brazilian. In a joint interview with her white domestic partner, she describes her lack of interest in the topic of slavery:

> *Tônica* My father spoke a lot about the time of slavery. I used to hear my father talk about this but I never had any interest in listening . . . And he used to tell stories. . . . We heard him talking to others about it, but never did I try to understand this. Because I thought "Ah, it ended. . . ."
>
> *FWT* Then your father knew a lot about slavery?
>
> *Tônica* Yes. He did.
>
> *FWT* Was your father a slave?
>
> *Tônica* Yes. He was. . . . but not all of his life. But only a part of his life was spent in slavery. . . . My grandfather used to say that he always wanted to eat good food but that only the rich people [white landowners] and the plantation owners were allowed to eat decent food. [Black slaves] used to eat cornmeal. . . . They ate the same thing as the animals.

Tônica's comments illustrate how she actively disregarded her father's attempts to transmit his memories of slavery to her. She rejected this knowledge and does not discuss the subject with her children. Tônica, an *empregada domestica* (domestic servant), is only one generation removed from the experience of slavery. As a domestic worker who earns approximately U.S.$25.00 per month for working seven days a week from 7:00 a.m. to 8:00 p.m., the social and material conditions of her life do not differ significantly from that of her slave ancestors. She does not earn enough to buy food, medicine, and other essentials for her family of five. In order to feed her children, she brings home the leftovers from the dinner table of her white middle-class employer.

Family Memories, Memorabilia, and the Erasure of African-Descent Ancestors

In the *sala* (living room), the family room where Dona Rosaria's family watches television each afternoon and the children play games, there is a cabinet that is used to store old editions of primary school textbooks, teaching supplies, and other miscellany. This cabinet also contains a cardboard box that holds more than two hundred photographs belonging to Dona Rosaria's family. One afternoon, Carla showed me these photographs and asked me to contribute one of myself to the collection.

These photographs provide some evidence of the paradoxes and tensions that emerge as aspiring working-class Afro-Brazilians attempt to negotiate the stigma of their African origins and their difficulties repositioning themselves as racially "unmarked" Brazilians. More than half of the photos visually document the vacations and interracial friendships of Dona Rosaria's daughter Helena, who has been living in the United States for more than a decade. In these photos, Helena is posed with various configurations of Europeans and European-Americans at dinners, birthday celebrations, and in front of monuments in European and North American countries. The photos document the upward mobility of Helena, and, by extension, of the entire family. They also suggest that the family's recently acquired image is contingent upon demonstrating to the community that they are linked to a family member who has been whitened by her associations in the United States.

Two of the photographs stand out from the others. They are striking because they show Helena at work as the empregada of elite Euro-Brazilians. In striking contrast to the others photos in which Helena is always smiling, in these she is frowning slightly with a look of sadness in her eyes. Holding a white child in her arms and looking very stiff, these photos appear to be a compulsory shot taken of Helena at the request of her employer. These pictures only hint at the price of mobility for Afro-Brazilian women who have few routes to upward mobility save for marriage, strategic sexual alliances, or migration to the larger urban cities as the domestic servants of elite white families.

Another set of photographs also reveal the contradictions between the self-representations of Helena's sisters, who never discuss their African ancestry, and how they are represented by the Euro-Brazilians in this community. As we were viewing the photographs, I came across one (circa 1981) of Shayla and her older sister Flora, dressed up in "African tribal costumes" in a parade. I asked Shayla to tell me the story of this. She frowned and said that they had been asked by the parade organizers to represent an African country in the city parade. This parade, which is held in April, is the Vasalian equivalent of Carnival, which is not celebrated in this community. Shayla and Flora had been invited to march as the representatives of Angola, the country that provided the Portuguese with a supply of African slave laborers during most of Brazil's history. The photo illustrates the difficulties that even light-skinned Afro-Brazilian women with hazel eyes have in erasing the symbolic link between themselves and their African ancestors. This photograph suggests that despite their efforts to distance themselves from their African ancestors and their use of race-evasive language when describing themselves, their participation in the parade was contingent upon their agreeing to represent traditional Africans.

There are no individuals of African descent in private family photo albums or photos displayed on the walls of the middle-class Euro-Brazilians I interviewed. Even among the elite, photography was so expensive until recently that only a few portraits of elites were commissioned and there are almost no photographic records of daily life prior to the 1930s. For example, Moema, the thirty-three-year-old granddaughter of one of the founding Portuguese families, has no photographs of herself as a child or even a teenager. The majority of residents have *pinturas*, illustrations found in most nonelite homes that are produced by local artists and that are more common than photographs.[10] Although working-class residents have only had access to commercial photography during the past fifteen years, some working-class families do have treasured black and white photos or pinturas of family members. These are typically the very small (1 x 1) black-and-white photos taken out of work registration books that employed Brazilians are required to carry. These books document their record of employment, wages, and all job titles held. In addition to the photo, the books show their date of birth, color, marital status, and education.

An analysis of the photo albums of Euro-Brazilians, like those of Afro-Brazilians, reveals how they also carefully construct and manage their family's self-representation so as to whiten their multiracial genealogy. In their descriptions of their genealogies, they typically minimize or deny that they have any African-descent ancestors. Thomas Skidmore reminds us: "The fact that Brazil had escaped the rigid application of the 'descent rule'—by which ancestry, not physical appearances (unless one passes for white) determines racial classification—should not be overemphasized. Origin could still be thought important in Brazil. Upwardly mobile mixed-bloods often took great pains to conceal their family background" ([1974] 1993, 40).

One day in May 1992, during a casual conversation with Miguel, a forty-something schoolteacher, he told me in private that he had recently discovered that his paternal great-grandmother had been married to a mulatto. He had always been told by his cousins and grandparents that his great grandfather had been a *bem moreno* (very dark-skinned) Indian but he had done some investigating and had determined that the man was actually the child of a black man and an Indian woman. He had become curious because dry, curly hair is a signifier of African ancestry and of blackness and he had noticed that his cousin has very curly hair. When he questioned his grandmother, she remained silent. Eventually he found some old photographs that were kept locked away at the home of his cousin, which confirmed his suspicions. He was not allowed to remove the photographs from the home or to have any reproductions made of them. He was only allowed to look at them briefly because he told his cousin that he wanted to see photos of his ancestors.

The photo album of Moema's sister-in-law, a Euro-Brazilian woman, described as a branca by everyone in the community, illustrates how African-descent relatives can be removed from the genealogies and photo albums of putatively all-white Euro-Brazilian elite families. Because of the nature of this practice it was impossible for me to determine how extensive this practice is among elite families. It suggests that despite the discourse of mestiçagem,

Brazilians place a high value on a lineage exclusive of African ancestry. The following excerpt is taken from my fieldnotes after visiting the home of Moema's sister-in-law.

> Monica, the wife of Moema's brother, is the daughter of an Italian man and a mulatta. Her maternal grandfather, who died recently at the age of ninety-nine, was born in Italy, and was forced to "marry" a black servant whom he impregnated while she was employed for his family. He was forced to flee his home in shame. However, after his death, no marriage documents were ever found so his family suspects that it was a common-law marriage not sanctioned by the church or state. They fled to this town after being expelled from his father's home in __. . . . This woman died at the young age of thirty-three after giving birth to four children with this man. According to the local gossip, during her lifetime, she was not allowed to leave the house or show her face at the window. Everyone was told by her mulatto children that she was their maid—not their mother. All evidence of this woman has been eliminated from the family photo album and other visual records kept for public viewing. Her photograph was removed from the family photo album. I discovered this when I asked to see a picture of her after having been told that at least one photo of her existed. I was told that there were no pictures of the grandmother. I was later told by the sister-in-law that pictures of her exist but they are *escondido* (hidden).

During another conversation, in the presence of his cousin Moema, Miguel commented on my curly hair and said that the *qualidade* (texture) was identical to one of his first cousins. Then he talked about recent discovery that his research on his genealogy had revealed. He told Moema that their great-grandfather was of African descent. Moema vehemently denied this and said that he had no proof. He said that he had seen a photograph while going through some old records. As he described his newly discovered ancestry, Moema became more and more visibly anxious and accused him of fabricating this story. In an interview with her later, when I asked her, "From what ethnic groups are you descended?" she later replied:

> I think, I am not certain, I am the descendants of Portuguese with Indians. Miguel has a better understanding of the genealogy of the

FIGURE 18. Dr. Giovanni and his wife, Raquel, members of the white elite of Vasalia. *(Photo by the author.)*

family. He said that we are descendants of the Puri Indians and the Portuguese. My grandmother. The mother of my father and her husband were Portuguese. Both were Portuguese. My maternal grandmother, the mother of my mother, was Portuguese and he [her grandfather] [long pause] I think that he was the descendant of a black but our family doesn't really know because he wasn't from this area. He was from Carangola. He came here, I don't know, from the city of Rio. She knew him only after he arrived here in Vasalia. She did not know the rest of his family, or where they lived. Thus, I don't really know if he has any African ancestry. But he was very dark. He resembled Miguel a little.

Moema was somewhat embarrassed as she talked about her paternal grandfather, who is of possible African ancestry. Like dark-skinned Afro-Brazilians who were asked about their African ancestry, she began crying in the middle of this interview and asked me to turn off the tape recorder so that she could collect herself. An analysis of the photo albums of five members of Moema's family enabled me to examine the range of phenotypes and color among their relatives and to note if any were of obvious African ancestry. I also noted which photos were prominently displayed and identified with pride. The photos that were kept hidden away in boxes and not displayed in the public family photo albums, the one shown to visitors, provided important information about who was claimed and named as family. All of my informants who had access to photos or pinturas of European-descent relatives tended to spend more time displaying them and discussing them with pride. Several poor black Brazilian farm laborers displayed a large photo of their Portuguese-Brazilian employer, for whom the entire family worked, on the first page of their family photo album.

As the case of Moema's maternal great-grandfather and of her sister-in-law's black mother illustrate, those relatives who were missing from the family photo album tended to be the African-descent mixed-race relatives of noticeable African and Indian ancestry. I was unable to determine the extent of this practice of hiding or destroying any visual evidence of African-descent ancestors, due to the taboo nature of this subject among the elite and middle whites. But I was able to confirm two cases of this within one of the eight elite families. Through extensive investigative work on his genealogy, Miguel, a descendant of a Portuguese founding family, had discovered that one of his great-grandparents was of black and Indian heritage. This individual was never mentioned to me by any other family member. Another female ancestor, the product of an affair between a "white" widow in the family and a black male servant, had also been erased from the family records. This woman had been given up for adoption and was not considered a member of the family.

One of the most critical distinctions white informants made was between relatives and ancestors born in Europe and those born in Brazil. Both Afro- and Euro-Brazilians tended to talk about their European-born or European-descent ancestors, and those who had light eyes [blue/green] and light hair were usually displayed more. Once in Brazil, it became more difficult for individuals to hold onto their racial purity, given the belief and reality of extensive race mixing.

Conclusion

What do children, particularly Afro-Brazilian children, learn from memorializing practices that overvalue white ancestors? In Vasalia children are taught to engage in practices that minimize their relation to African and Afro-Brazilian ancestors while privileging their relationship to Europeans and European ancestors. By distancing themselves from their African-descent ancestors, Afro-Brazilians actively sustain white supremacy.

A whiter identity is constructed in federal census records, community histories, and in family genealogies of Vasalians. The whitening practices that I documented in this chapter actively support the Brazilian national project of embranquecimento. Afro-Brazilians, as slaves and later as freed laborers, are typically erased in multiracial family genealogies, birth registration records, primary and secondary school lessons, and for middle-class and upwardly mobile multiracial families, they may be removed from their family photo albums.

Afro-Brazilians are also excluded from the local history lessons. This produces a public collective memory that erases slavery from this region, denying Vasalia's reliance on slave labor. Although members of the Euro-Brazilian elite know that slavery occurred (because they possess family documents that list the African slaves their ancestors once owned), this is not something that they voluntarily discuss or teach their children. Children in Vasalia do not learn the history of local slavery or its legacy—reflected in the current economic, political, and social subordination of Afro-Brazilians.

Finally, family memories and narratives are important sites for antiracism as reflected by practices in which both elite and nonelite families construct a whiter past by emphasizing their connection to European ancestors. I found that oral and visual histories are constructed in ways that are antiblack, particularly when the *preferred readings* of family photo albums are analyzed in Afro- and Euro-Brazilian homes. In white elite families, European-descent family members are visually displayed while individuals bearing evidence of African ancestry are kept hidden; Afro-Brazilian families claim a multiracial heritage, but elite Euro-Brazilian families reject this narrative of mestiçagem.

CHAPTER 7

Strategic Responses to Racism

PRESERVING WHITE SUPREMACY

I ignore racism when it occurs.
—Dr. Rodolpho

What do I do when I see racism? . . . I pretend that I am not listening because I don't want to discuss it. I ignore [racist comments] because I don't want to give them a chance to start an argument with me.
—Monisha

I choose the places I go, and I don't insist on going where I don't fit. First I try to find out what kind of place it is, and what type of person is likely to be present. . . . I'm not going to upset a situation that, for better or worse, is good.
—Former Afro-Brazilian São Paulo city council representative
(quoted in Andrews 1991, 176)

A main strategy of the Black movement has been to denounce Brazilian racial inequalities and to point out the racial discrimination felt by non-White people in everyday, ordinary situations. These episodes of racial discrimination are often hidden and hard to identify, are never punished, and are not publicly recognized as racial prejudice.
—Rosana Heringer (1996, 204)

*T*his chapter analyzes the responses of Afro-Brazilian Vasalians to acts that they define as racist. I begin by providing a typology of their responses to everyday racism. I then analyze the efficacy of these strategies in challenging Euro-Brazilian domination. It will be evident that the strategies employed by Afro-Brazilian professionals leaves intact white supremacy because orthodox discourses that define social discrimination as a simple consequence of socioeconomic inequality are not challenged. Further, Afro-Brazilians respond to racism in ways that fail to challenge the mythology of *democracia racial*, which denies the ongoing and pervasive racism that Afro-Brazilians encounter. Thus, the repertoire of responses I will examine preserves *racismo cordial* (polite racism), and fails to call into question or alter racist practices.

Responses to Racism in the Public Sphere

In public discussions and in private conversations, *brincadeiras* (jokes) emerged as an important vehicle for transmitting racist stereotypes. Afro-Brazilians interviewed reported that they are routinely subjected to brincadeiras of a racist nature. These jokes typically involved the body parts of Afro-Brazilians being compared to a *macaca* (monkey). Euro-Brazilians also reported that comparing the body parts (hair, nose, mouth) of Afro-Brazilians to that of animals is a common practice. In Vasalia, joking is a socially acceptable way to articulate beliefs publicly and reproduce white supremacy and black inferiority. Analyzing the significance of racist jokes in the reproduction of racist structures, British geographer Peter Jackson argues:

> The reproduction of racist ideologies similarly involves a range of social practices from overt aspects of public policy to more mundane features of everyday life. For even such an apparently inoffensive action as telling a "racist" or ethnic joke serves to reinforce existing prejudices and actively reproduces the unequal social relations upon which more instrumental forms of racism are based . . . and racist jokes are one type of social practices that is both a medium for the reproduction of racist structures and an outcome of the structural racism that characterizes our society. (1987, 10)

Ariana describes an incident that illustrates the forms that racist jokes may take in this region. Her response to the joke also reflects how Afro-Brazilian professionals respond to this form of public racism.

> They were good friends of mine. I say "were" because they have already died. They were my wedding godparents, the ones who witnessed the wedding and sign the wedding documents. At that time,

I was no longer a girl, I was already married. So they went to serve themselves. When they came [to the dining area] and saw a bunch of bananas, [my white godfather] took the bunch of bananas from the table. The hotel was full of people and the worst thing is that it was Sunday [. . .] all these tourists were there. And when I sat down at the table and was enjoying my meal, I will never forget this. I was eating ham with bread, something that I had never eaten that early in the day before. [My white godfather] screamed at the table. "Come see the bananas, take a banana, the preferred food of Dinha." That was the object of derision for the rest of my life. Because he left that table and saw the table where I was sitting and placed the banana in front of me. And the people who heard him speaking in a loud voice went looking to see who Dinha was. When they saw that it was me, and that a banana was in his hand, and that I was black . . . What did they think? A monkey? Ah, they cracked up. They laughed so hard! And what could I do?

What is significant here is not the joke but Ariana's response to this racial abuse. The "joke" draws on racist stereotypes that link the food preferences and physical characteristics of dark-skinned Afro-Brazilians to that of monkeys. Although the racism in this comment is contained by their laughter and appears to be merely a joke, Ariana interprets the comments as racist. But she responds in silence and does *not* reframe the joke as racist. Her silence does not disrupt the public discourse of racial democracy or the culture of racismo cordial but leaves dominant definitions of social reality intact.

Ariana's response is typical of what I witnessed during my field research. Passive responses to these routine racist practices fail to effectively challenge either the racist *content* of this joke or the *practice* of engaging in jokes that reflect and circulate racist ideologies. Like other middle-class Afro-Brazilian professionals who reported being teased in this way, Ariana did not challenge the behavior of whites but instead dramatically altered her behavior to avoid being humiliated again. Since this incident, which occurred more than seven years ago, Ariana never inspects, eats, or purchases bananas in public. She has also carefully taught her six-year-old daughter, who bears a striking resemblance to her, to never examine, touch, or eat bananas in public for fear that she will be subjected to this form of racial abuse.

Dr. Rodolpho, one of four medical doctors in Vasalia, is the highest-paid Afro-Brazilian in this community. He moved to Vasalia nine years ago, at the age of twenty-six, to accept a position at the hospital and, according to his neighbors, he maintains a high degree of social distance and has established no close friendships. When explicitly asked about racism in his professional life, Dr. Rodolpho denied that he had ever experienced any racism in Vasalia. He further said that it does not exist here. Although in a private interview he denied that racism personally affected him, he later added: "[Whites] said things, sometimes in joking, but there was a *little* racism in this, right? From the moment that you compare a black person to a monkey, I think that there is some discrimination occurring." At another point in the interview, Dr. Rodolpho acknowledged that jokes of a racist nature were made on a daily basis. "It happens daily. If a person with white skin has a disagreement with a dark-skinned person, they say "nigger" or "black." . . . It could be a joke, but it contains a little racism, doesn't it?" Notice that while acknowledging that racist jokes are told daily, Dr. Rodolpho contains his criticism by saying, "It could be a joke," and he modifies the word racism, with "little."

Dr. Giovanni is a white medical doctor who works at the same hospital as Dr. Rodolpho. In a separate private conversation, he contradicted Dr. Rodolpho's statements. In the following excerpt from a private taped conversation, Dr. Giovanni provides a specific example of the routine racial abuse that he witnessed daily:

> Whenever [Dr. Rodolpho] makes a mistake in the moment of anger, any time there is an emotional explosion, the first thing that the white employees and patients say is this: "That black. That animal, with his large nose," in a pejorative manner. . . . No one can use my physical characteristics as something that could offend me . . . to use my appearance as weapons against me, in offensive terms. [This occurs] always in the moment of a fight. And with Dr. Rodolpho, any time [he is not perfect] the first thing that the person will say is this, "Why do you have to be so black? Why are you such an animal?"

Dr. Rodolpho's silence illustrates again how Afro-Brazilians, even middle-class professionals, typically respond to the racism they encounter. Rather than publicly challenging racist behavior, they respond with silence.

These two cases reflect how racist acts continue to occur in public without Vasalians being held accountable for these racist practices.

The Unspeakable in the Public and Private Sphere

There are few subjects, if any, in Vasalia that are more difficult to discuss in private or public than racism. During my field research I never witnessed anyone initiate or engage in public discussions of racial inequality. When I attempted to raise this issue, I was immediately silenced by residents who accused me of being a racist for simply calling attention to what I perceived to be racial disparities in employment, education, housing, and political representation.

During a private conversation that took place in her home one evening, Raquel, the thirty-one-year-old great-granddaughter of Italian-Brazilian plantation owners who settled in this region of Vasalia in the 1840s, described the limits of acceptable local discourse. She characterizes the public and private etiquette in Vasalia: "Today people do not want to acknowledge that [racial inequality] exists, understand? Precisely because everyone is so conscious of racial difference, they do not want to admit to being aware of racism. They are ashamed to admit that they are racists. Normally this is the case. But in their hearts I believe that the majority of [whites] society carries this *preconceito* (prejudice) within them this racism against [blacks]."

The Afro-Brazilians I interviewed all reported that they had *never* discussed their experiences of racism with their family members or friends. I lived with a working-class Afro-Brazilian family for ten months. During the entire time of my field research I never heard them mention racism or engage in serious discussions of racial inequality. When I asked if they had ever discussed this incident with their family, *none* reported having ever discussed racism with any of their family members or friends. What is surprising is that even in their homes, a private space where they do not have to fear white retaliation, they still do not engage in discussions that could assist their family members and themselves in collectively coping with racism.

In a comparative analysis of everyday racism experienced by U.S. black women and Surinamese women living in the Netherlands, Philomena Essed found that U.S. black women are advantaged in coping with racism because "they had the advantage of a large body of relevant literature." Essed also found that U.S. black women had acquired extensive knowledge about racism from their families as children.

> The facts of racial inequality were known in the families and communicated to the children. . . . A few women came from families where both parents had a college education. In these families the parents valued discussion as an important method of socializing their children. Therefore the women recall the explicit guidance and support to identify with the Black cause and to fight against the forces of racism. . . . Because the impact of antiracism in education and the media is still marginal, informal communication of knowledge about racism, in particular within the family is highly relevant. . . . It may be assumed that family attitudes on racism largely determine the social perceptions of Black children. (1991, 94)

Children in Vasalia do not hear their parents, teachers, or associates discuss racism. Having grown up as a black child in the United States, I was accustomed to racism being a daily topic of conversation, especially in private arenas. Thus, it was quite surprising to me that racism was never discussed while I lived in the home of working-class Afro-Brazilians. In a context in which I was subjected to a high degree of racism every day, my adopted family constantly told me that I had "misinterpreted" someone's statements or actions. I was also told on numerous occasions that it was inappropriate for me to raise this issue, particularly in the presence of children.

When asked if he had ever been subjected to racist treatment, Tomas, a thirty-seven-year-old dark-skinned Afro-Brazilian (who refers to himself as a negro), replied, "I would be rich if I were white and had the same personality." He pointed to his excellent social skills, his ambition, and the lack of rewards he receives because of the racism he encounters as a dark-skinned black man. Although he recognized racism as a factor that restricted his ability to acquire the same material resources as his white counterparts, he offered no critique of institutional racism and framed his encounters with racism as an "individual" problem.

When asked whether he ever recounted to his wife or children his experiences with racism, Tomas replied, "I never discuss the problems of racism at home. Never." When asked if he was preparing his youngest daughter, a dark-skinned preta, to cope with racism, he replied that "she will learn how to manage [racism] on her own." Like the other Afro-Brazilians I spoke to about this topic, he does not actively prepare his children to develop effective strategies to challenge the racism they encounter.

Seclusion and Self-Segregation

Another common response to racism in the public sphere is withdrawal and self-segregation.[1] Cristiano, a loquacious thirty-one-year-old Afro-Brazilian ambulance driver, is married to the white daughter of ranchers. He is the father of two sons of salient African ancestry. Like many Vasalians, he supplements his income during the summer months by working part time in the city of Rio de Janeiro. He described the events that led to his decision to leave his position as a driver for a tourist company.

> I worked at a tourist agency. This firm was Argentinean. My boss was white [Brazilian]. The guy who used to work there from Vasalia was also white. We grew up together. This is what happened. I am a very charismatic person and I try to make friends with people. During the first month of work, I used to pick up the tourists at the airport. Jose brought them to the hotel and I would take them to the beach resorts. I worked there for three months. The first month that I worked there, all of the passengers who entered my van talked with me. Then I would take them from the airport to their hotel. . . . When they returned, the same people that I drove from the airport would ask for me specifically, to provide that same service again. When I arrived, this white guy said, "Look the couple that you brought to the Hotel Chelton called. They want you to take them to the Angels dos Reis." I said, OK. The third time that they requested me, this [Italian-Brazilian] guy, the owner, looked for me and said, "Look, you cannot do this with the passengers. I said, "Why not?" He said, "You cannot continue to socialize with the customers. You are talking to them too much." I began to think, "Why can't I talk to the tourists?" They are arriving in Brazil for the first time. I am the driver. I have to remain quiet. I can't talk. Then he said, "No, you can't talk to the customers because we have a tour guide to provide this service." I know that when there are many passengers, they have to ask the guide. So when the guide came I used to remain quiet. I didn't

say anything but when there was no tour guide present, I spoke with them. I also speak a little Spanish. I make friendships easily. I began to suspect that this white man, this white [supervisor] began to get scared. He realized that the tourists were on very close terms with me. . . . The white owner had too much fear.

Why was he afraid of me? I brought him more business. Stop talking to the tourists that bring the boss business. He remained afraid of my success. I believe that if whites think that a person of color is surpassing them, they begin to act crazy. I believe that this is true. White co-workers were afraid that I would replace them.

Cristiano argued that he would have surpassed his Euro-Brazilian colleagues in both earnings and occupational mobility if he had not been subjected to racism because he is more competent and socially skilled than his white co-workers. Instead of being rewarded for his skills, he was penalized by white supervisors. Cristiano subsequently quit this job rather than directly challenge his boss. In a separate private conversation that I had with his white wife, she told me that Cristiano never discussed his reasons for leaving this position. She added that during their ten years of marriage he had never discussed racism with her or their children.

Here we see that Afro-Brazilians respond to racism by withdrawing, rather than by discussing their experiences with their family members in private conversations. This silence does not generate a discursive space in which they can teach their children strategies for coping with racism. Ultimately, this strategy of individually managing the racism alone and in silence sustains the fiction that racism is an isolated and individual problem rather than an endemic problem.

Another example of withdrawal as a response to racism in their professional life can be taken from an experience that an Afro-Brazilian teacher reported to me involving Dr. Rodolpho. In 1992, when the first mayor was elected, he gained control over the city budget, which had previously been under the jurisdiction of Boa Vista. It was revealed that the combined salaries of the four doctors constituted almost 50 percent of the hospital's budget. Instead of discussing reducing the salary of all four doctors, the mayor threatened to dismiss the one black doctor. Adriano, an Afro-Brazilian teacher, and others took steps to ensure that Dr. Rodolpho was not terminated. They circulated a petition and distributed it among the residents testifying to the excellent service and medical treatment that they had received from Dr. Rodolpho. "In the case of Dr. Rodolpho, he wanted to leave town because he had problems with the mayor. We made a petition and signed it asking him not to leave because he is one of the best doctors that this city has. He is a general practitioner and he provides services to *everyone* who comes. We sent this petition to the mayor in order to keep him in his position as a city employee."

It is very likely that if the citizens of Vasalia had not intervened, the sole Afro-Brazilian doctor would have resigned from his position rather than directly challenging the mayor for targeting him to be fired. What is most informative about this is that Dr. Rodolpho never mentioned to me that his job had been in jeopardy and he denied that he had ever been subjected to any racism.

In a historical study of black and white workers in São Paulo, George Reid Andrews notes that successful blacks usually avoid conflict:

> Many middle-class Afro-Brazilians, who have expended tremendous effort to achieve some measure of success in Brazilian society, do not wish to endanger that success by confronting racism head-on. Such confrontations are always risky and unpleasant, and, in the opinion of many blacks, are unlikely to improve the racial climate in Brazil . . . much of the Black middle-class try to avoid situations in which they are likely to encounter white racism, and thus minimize its impact on their daily life. (1991, 176)

Like Andrews, I also found that in Rio de Janeiro conflict avoidance is a preferred strategy for managing racism among Afro-Brazilians of all classes. Afro-Brazilians who are economically able to live in close residential proximity to Euro-Brazilians restrict their exposure to the middle class by engaging in *self-segregation*. Whatever their motives, this practice of minimizing the potential for acts of racism helps produce racial harmony while sustaining white supremacy. The self-segregation of Afro-Brazilians protects them from potentially painful acts of racism while simultaneously allowing the Euro-Brazilian middle and upper class to maintain racially exclusive social events without being publicly challenged. Thus, some de facto social segregation by race continues in Vasalia even as the dominant fiction of racial equality remains intact.[2]

Isabela, an upper-middle-class Euro-Brazilian business owner, commented on the racial segregation in Vasalian social life. She described the absence of Afro-Brazilians at the city's social events in a way that maintains her innocence and that of other Euro-Brazilian elites who routinely discriminate against Afro-Brazilians. She does not acknowledge that ongoing racial discrimination, however subtle, might be partially responsible for the self-segregation of Afro-Brazilians in Vasalia. "I think that here [in comparison to the city of Rio] blacks isolate themselves more [from whites], understand? They don't go to certain places where whites go. So much so that they don't attend the parties, the dances, the so-called society events of Vasalia. Anyone who pays at the door is allowed to enter."

This self-segregation minimizes potential conflicts and protects Afro-Brazilians from racism. They avoid situations in which they perceive a high risk of racial discrimination, such as being the sole nonwhite at an elite event. Afro-Brazilians try to limit their social contacts outside of work to "safe" individuals such as family members, friends, associates, and others who will behave in a polite and race-evasive manner. They minimize encounters with overt forms of racism in Vasalia by socializing within their extended family network.

Dr. Rodolpho and Senhor Fernando are the sole Afro-Brazilian physician and lawyer in this community. Senhor Fernando, who has a degree in law, has never practiced law but operates a gas station in the neighboring town that he purchased from the previous white owner. Based on my observations and interviews with the town residents, I documented a pattern of self-seclusion in which both of these men actively restricted their contact with residents to formal business relationships. They interacted with local residents only in their roles as service providers and avoided virtually all nonprofessional social contact with them. Neither reported any close friendships with residents.

An analysis of Dr. Rodolpho's travel patterns will illustrate how he attempts to protect himself from racist encounters. He is never seen walking in the community, except when he is required to attend an event at the home of his supervisor. Dr. Morelli, who lives across the street from him, told me

F<small>IGURE</small> 19. Looking down the hill. A view from the hospital looking down toward the main street. Dr. Rudolpho never walks on this street, but will travel on it only by car. *(Photo by the author)*

that Dr. Rodolpho traveled to his job at the hospital by car every day. This is unusual because all of the white doctors who live the same distance from the hospital walk to work. Given that the hospital is at most a five-minute walk from his home, this is noteworthy. In contrast to all of his white colleagues at the hospital, I also never saw Dr. Rodolpho walk *anywhere* in town. In addition to not walking, I never saw him casually interacting with the local residents on the street and he appeared to be very uncomfortable when outside of the hospital. Thus, when Dr. Rodolpho interacted with Vasalians, it was in his professional role as a physician. Virtually every weekend, Dr. Rodolpho drove his family out of town on vacations or to visit family in his home town.

In a similar vein, neighbors reported to me that Dr. Rodolpho had never invited any of them into his home during his nine years of residence. They were so anxious to gain access to his fairly new two-story home that Moema and several of her white middle-class cousins tried to persuade me to help

FIGURE 20. Moema (front, left) and her siblings, members of the white elite. *(Photo by Jonathan Warren.)*

them gain social access to his home during one of my scheduled interviews with him. However, Dr. Rodolpho would only agree to be interviewed at his office in the hospital and he never invited me to enter his home. I was told that during his nine years of residence in Vasalia, he had cultivated no close friendships with anyone in the community. The only social events he attended were obligatory rituals held by the other medical doctors who hired him.

These practices suggest that the class privileges and class status of Dr. Rodolpho are contingent upon his self-seclusion and silence. It is evident that his class does not protect Dr. Rodolpho from the racism of Vasalians. Although these practices are not theorized as ways to manage everyday racism, previous researchers have documented similar practices among the rare Afro-Brazilian professional present at a white elite event. Marvin Harris describes the behavior of a middle-class black politician in a rural town in northeastern Brazil in the early 1950s.

> At upper-class parties and dances he keeps in the background. When
> invited to be seated to have coffee and cake with the rest of the guests,
> he invariably declines and takes his refreshments standing. No one
> ever insists too much. The solicitude which is shown him as a coun-

cilman in such circumstances depends entirely on the certainty that he will not accept too much of it—that he knows his place, in other words. Though he is invited to most formal upper-class functions, he never visits their homes and they never visit his. (1952, 68)

Harris's description of a black councilman in the 1950s bears a strong resemblance to the behavior of Senhor Fernando, whom according to his daughter, Ariana, "routinely receives invitations to the weddings, funerals, and birthday celebrations of the elites but *never* attends." When I accompanied Moema to white elite events, I was always told that one or two Afro-Brazilian professionals had been invited but declined to attend because they had other obligations.

Another example of this practice of self-seclusion among the most educated and financially secure Afro-Brazilian professionals in Vasalia can be illustrated by an incident that occurred after my interview with Senhor Fernando. One Sunday morning, I arrived with his daughter, Ariana, tape recorder in hand, to conduct a private interview about racial inequality. After spending the entire morning conducting an in-depth life history interview with Senhor Fernando, I was hungry. As four o'clock approached, I asked Senhor Fernando if there were any restaurants in town that served fish. I had been eating black beans and white rice every day for more than five months and wanted to taste another variation of the local cuisine. I adore fish and shared this information with Senhor Fernando. He generously offered to give me a tour of the neighborhood that he grew up in and then to take me to a local, moderately priced restaurant that specialized in fish.

As we entered the restaurant, I began to engage in my usual racial mapping, quickly assessing the ratio of white to nonwhite customers in the restaurant, hoping that this place would be different from the city of Rio de Janeiro where I was typically the *only* person of color (and often the only woman) seated at a dining table. I was not surprised to find no Afro-Brazilians of any shade in this establishment. Ariana, who had been carefully observing me since we entered the restaurant, suspected that I was mentally recording everything so that I could write it down later. She and her father took me over to the restaurant owner, a branco, and introduced me. I suspected that this was a courtesy and a warning (for him) so that he wouldn't mistake me for a Brazilian and treat me rudely. When she told him that I was an American and was here to study racism, he looked very uncomfortable and immediately said, "We don't have *that* problem here." I politely said, "Yes, so I've been told," and proceeded to watch the door to see if any Afro-Brazilians or other nonwhites entered during our meal.

Two hours later, we remained the only multiracial table of customers (three pretas, a mulatta, and a branco); not a single *pessoa de cor* (colored person) had entered during that time. At one point, the owner (who was also one of the waiters that evening) caught me looking around. He glanced around the room nervously and a moment later hurried over to our table to ask me if I was enjoying my meal and offered me the following information: "Blacks and mulattos don't come here on Sundays." I asked, "When do they come?" He replied, "*No segunda-feiras*" (On Mondays). I then asked him how many of his customers are typically people of color. He quickly replied, "*Meia-meia*"(fifty/fifty).

Two weeks later, I asked one of the local white politicians (also a wealthy plantation owner) to accompany me to dinner at this same restaurant. This would provide me with an opportunity to determine if Afro-Brazilians did frequent this restaurant on week nights. Once again we arrived around 6:00 p.m., and there wasn't a single Afro-Brazilian in the place. During the four-hour meal none entered. The waiter nervously laughed and told me that I kept coming on the "wrong" days. I later learned from his daughter that Fernando had never in his sixty-seven years of residence in this community eaten in this or any other local restaurant. If he wanted to take his family to a restaurant he would leave town and go to another community. Thus, he avoided any situations in which he might cause discomfort to the local Euro-Brazilian middle class or elites by entering *their* social space.

Restricting their social contact with white elites to obligatory events is an effective strategy for minimizing encounters with racism. However, this practice fails to challenge the behavior of white elites, who continue to hold de facto white-only events while paying lip service to the public discourse of democracia racial. If, as middle-class professionals Afro-Brazilians were mistreated at middle-class events, they could directly challenge the discourse of class inequality that I described in previous chapters (see Chapter Four). George Reid Andrews (1991) also argues that this practice effectively helps to sustain white domination.

Many [Afro-Brazilians], when confronted by an overt act of racism, try to explain it away, look for excuses, erase it—but its mark stays on you, influencing even the choice of a career and of what places to go into and stay away from.

By persuading Afro-Brazilians to lower their expectations in life and not to create "disagreeable situations" by trying to push into places where they're not wanted (i.e., places which whites wish to reserve for themselves), the Brazilian model of race relations works very effectively to reduce racial tension and competition while maintaining blacks in a subordinate social and economic position. Indeed, the obstacles are seen as so formidable that the only way they can triumph is by turning themselves into superhumans. (1992, 175)

This pattern of self-segregation and avoidance of situations in which they anticipate being rejected because of their color is further illustrated by the comments of Maria, a forty-year-old teacher. Maria rarely, if ever, attends any social events that occur outside of the homes of family members. In discussing past negative experiences in a public bar in town, Maria blamed herself for feeling uncomfortable in public multiracial milieus. "Look, Francine, I didn't used to frequent that place [white social club] because I knew that I was going to be barred from entering. Even if I had been 'Cinderella,' I was going to be prevented from entering because I was black, the child of my father . . . and when I began to frequent bars with my [white] husband, I began to feel a little shame, in certain places. But I think that it was my own problem."

Like other Afro-Brazilians interviewed, Maria interprets her experience as an *individual* problem. She blames herself for her feelings of discomfort in public spaces that are controlled by whites. Like other Afro-Brazilians interviewed, Maria actively restricts her social interactions and avoids going to social events where she anticipates being subjected to any social discrimination. Maria protects herself from racial harassment by not attempting to participate fully in the public life of the community. She minimizes her encounters with racism, so she is rarely in situations where she is likely to encounter it. When confronted with overt racism, Maria, like other Afro-Vasalians interviewed, said that she never directly challenges the racist practices of other Vasalians.

In Chapter Three, I discussed the racism encountered by Afro-Brazilians who attempt to join the Village Country Club. Recall that Tatiana described the obstacles to membership that middle-class blacks face. Those dark-skinned Afro-Brazilians who were not denied membership often faced subtle forms of social exclusion and voluntarily withdrew from the club. Although Ariana's father continued to pay for this membership, she never goes to the Village Social Club nor does she participate in any events sponsored by it. However, as she still officially belongs, the club administrators can claim that there is no racial discrimination there.

Containing the "Shock": Defending Harmonious Relations

The silence and seclusion of Afro-Brazilian professionals in response to racism in the public sphere is important when theorizing about the maintenance of white supremacy in Brazil because their class places them in a strategic position to *challenge* white domination and thus to alter the behavior of white elites. In contrast to working-class Afro-Brazilians, they are not explicitly prohibited from entering social, educational, and occupational spaces (milieus that typically include people of color only as servants) on the basis of their socioeconomic position. Once in these milieus, they could call attention to the discrepancies between the ideal of racial egalitarianism and the realities of racism.

How can we explain the silence of Afro-Brazilians in the public and private spheres? Coercion or fear of retaliation cannot adequately explain the failure of Afro-Brazilians to directly challenge racism, to not discuss their experiences with their family members. What does this self-segregation and silence accomplish? I will argue that it preserves harmonious relations that ultimately leave white supremacy intact. In her analysis of the criteria that Guyanese use in their status evaluations, Brackette Williams suggests another form of containment accomplished by the self-segregation and silence of Afro-Brazilians around racism.

> Disjunctions between expectations that synchronize the potential for individual status achievements and ethnic identity result in what Cockalorums refer to as "getting a shock." This shock is experienced when persons confront a situation in which another person's achieve-

ments and apparent status greatly outstrip or fail to live up to expectations based on his ethnic identity. For example, East Indian informants reported getting a shock when confronted with Africans
whose material worth they judged not only equal to but greater than
appearance would suggest. This shock was most jarring when they
could find no proof that the African had adopted some other ethnic
culture.(1991, 177)

Employing the Guyanese concept of "getting a shock" is one way of
theorizing how Afro-Brazilian professionals attempt to preserve racial harmony by containing the shock that their achievements may cause Euro-
Brazilian elites. Furthermore, silence and self-seclusion allow Afro-Brazilian
professionals to manage the contradictions between their elevated class status and their inferior racial status. Afro-Brazilians actively maintain harmonious relations with white elites by minimizing the anxiety and disruption
that their status achievements generate in the local community.

Working in an urban community among working-class Afro-Brazilians
in the city of Rio de Janeiro, the U.S. white anthropologist Robin Sheriff
(1997) found a pattern of silence around the topic of racism. The consequences of this pattern of silence is that realities of racism remain submerged
and racism is a "disallowed" topic, thus supporting the ideology of democracia
racial. By discussing their experiences, Afro-Brazilians professionals could
generate awareness among working-class Brazilians who, if they are not aware
of the racism directed at more privileged Afro-Brazilians, continue to interpret acts of social discrimination as being only those of class inequality.

An example of the type of shock that the presence of an Afro-Brazilian
professional can generate at elite events can be illustrated by my experience
as the only nonwhite at an elite event. Moema invited me to attend the 100th
anniversary celebration of the largest coffee plantation in this region. When
I arrived, I found that I was the only nonwhite guest among approximately
two hundred guests. The only Afro-Brazilians present were children of plantation workers. Moema told me that two prominent black (male) Afro-Brazilians had been invited (including Dr. Rodolpho), but they had declined to
attend. My presence generated shock, silence, and hostile stares. I found myself treated as a "nonperson."[3] With the exception of the white wife of a famous black soccer player (who did not attend), no one engaged in any eye

contact or conversation with me. At one point, I posed a direct question about the history of the plantation to the forty-something son of the plantation owner as he visited our dining table. In response, he turned away from me and gave a reply to my white partner, never engaging in eye contact with me nor acknowledging that I had asked him a question.

The self-seclusion in which Dr. Rodolpho and Senhor Fernando engage protects them from this type of humiliation and mundane forms of racism that I experienced whenever I attended middle-and upper-class social events. For example, the white family members of my white associates often assumed that I was the new *empregada*. This seemed to be the only rational explanation for my presence in white middle-class households or events. In fact, on several occasions, my friend Moema would anxiously approach her relatives and explain to them before they were introduced to me that although I "looked like a *brasileira mesma*" (real Brazilian) I was really a North American and should *not* be treated like an Afro-Brazilian. This was a thinly veiled request to treat me as an honorary white since her family told me that they had no *social* acquaintances who were not white and that people of color entered their homes as domestic servants.

In previous chapters (see Chapter Four) I argued that Vasalians rationalize racial disparities by arguing that class oppression is responsible for the subordination of Afro-Brazilians. It is clear from my experiences and from what Afro-Vasalians described in private that "money doesn't whiten," because Afro-Brazilian professionals in Vasalia are not treated as "honorary whites." Moreover, their experiences of racism contradict the orthodox public discourses of racial democracy in this community. As a medical doctor, Dr. Rodolpho possesses a degree of material wealth and education that one would expect to shield him from the type of racial abuse that less-privileged and poorer Afro-Brazilians encounter. However, his white colleagues reported that, despite his upper-middle-class economic status, he was routinely subjected to the same kind of verbal racial abuse that less-privileged dark-skinned Brazilians also reported.

Conclusion

None of the Afro-Brazilians I knew in Vasalia discuss racism with their children. Their silence, although strategic for the purposes of retaining employment and sustaining harmonious relations with the white elite, ultimately sustains white domination. These responses disempower Afro-Brazilian children and adolescents, who learn that their experiences with racism are a taboo subject for discussion with their parents or peers. Previous research in Brazil suggests that the experiences and life chances of children *within the same families* vary on the basis of how closely their appearance reflects salient European ancestry (Patai 1988; Scheper-Hughes 1992). The information that parents provide to their children about how to respond to racism is critical in helping the children to acquire effective strategies for coping with various forms of racism (Essed 1991, 99). Lacking a comprehensive body of children's and young adult antiracist literature, an antiracist education curriculum in schools, and a familial context in which this subject is taboo in private discussions, Afro-Brazilian children usually have no discursive spaces to learn to *collectively* challenge racist ideologies and practices.

In a milieu that denies (and minimizes) the reality of everyday racism, it remains virtually impossible for Afro-Brazilian youth to gain access to or to generate an antiracist consciousness or effective antiracist discourses or practices that could empower them in the face of white supremacy. If their parents, teachers, priests, politicians, and peers continue to avoid discussions of the realities of racial inequality, will they simply reproduce a society morally committed to the ideal of racial egalitarianism while allowing racism to continue? The future of the Brazilian racial democracy ultimately depends upon the ability of the next generation to confront the realities of racism.

The strategies Afro-Brazilian adults employ to manage the racism they encounter (or anticipate) have a particular impact on their children since adults are responsible for providing children with the conceptual tools and skills to survive in society. Discursive and material practices that "disallow" discussions of racism remain obstacles that make it very difficult for Brazilian youth to acquire or develop an antiracist consciousness and antiracist discourses in Vasalia, leaving intact the ideal of the racial democracy and the reality of white supremacy.

Appendix A

Interview Schedule

1. Describe a typical day in your life. What is your daily routine? Describe your activities from the time you wake up until you retire to bed.
2. From what sources do you receive the majority of your information about events in Brazil?
3. Describe those physical characteristics that you find most attractive. Could you provide an example of the type of person you find beautiful?
4. Do you attend church? If, yes, which church? How frequently?
5. How would you define the term branco (white)?
6. How would you define the term negro/preto (black)?
7. Could you explain how you determine someone's racial identity?
8. How would you define racism? Could you provide specific examples of what you would consider an act of racism?
9. As a child growing up, what did you learn about racism from your family? From friends? Could you provide a specific example?
10. What were you explicitly taught about racial inequality at school? Explain.
11. Have you thought about what you are going to teach your children about racism? If you currently have children, what have you taught them about racism?
12. Do you (or have you) ever discussed racism with your friends? Explain.
13. Is racism the subject of conversations today in your social circle?
14. Do you think that racism exists here in Vasalia? Why? Could you provide a specific example?

15. Have you ever personally encountered racism? Explain the circumstances. Have you ever encountered racism outside of Vasalia?

16. If yes to question 15, could you describe how you responded to this act of racism?

17. Do you have any other examples of racism that you have not personally encountered that you would like to share?

18. Do you know any wealthy people here? Are any of them people of color? Are any black?

19. Do you know any plantation owners? Are any of them people of color? Are any black?

20. Do you know any Catholic priests? Are any of them people of color? Any black?

21. Do you know any middle-class blacks?

22. Do you know any middle-class whites married to blacks?

23. Do you know any middle-class whites who married poor whites? Please provide specific examples.

24. How would you explain the absence of people of color among the elite of Vasalia?

25. Do you know any poor whites married to blacks or mulattos?

26. Do you know any people of color who live on the main street?

27. Among the city council representatives, how many are white and non-white? Explain.

28. What problems do you think poor whites and people of color encounter? Are there are any similarities or differences in the problems that poor whites and people of color encounter? Explain.

29. Do you personally know any blacks or mulattos who dislike whites? Explain.

30. Do you know any blacks who dislike blacks and mulattos? Could you provide an example?

31. Do you know any whites who dislike people of color? Could you provide a specific example?

32. How do you think that your life might be different if you were a wo/man?

33. How do you think your life might be different, if you were white/non-white?

34. You are the descendant of which ethnic/racial groups? Explain.

Appendix B

Biographical Data on Interviewees

Name	Age	Occupation	Color	Marital Status	Color of Partner	Salary
Monisha	17	Student	White	S	Black	None
Sueli	18	Maid	Black	S	White	0.5
Margarida	19	Student	Morena	S	White	None
Carla	21	Teacher	Mul./Black	S	NA	2.5
Eduardo	21	Military	Mul.	S	Black	2.0
Aida	21	Housewife	Morena	M	Black	0.5
Jorge	22	Clerk	Mul.	S	White	1.5
Carlucci	23	Clerk	Mul./Black	S	White	1.0
Pedro	23	Student	White	S	NA	2.0
Camillo	26	Gardener	Mul./Black	S	NA	Unreported
Carlos	27	Basketmaker	White	C	Black	0.5
Mani	27	Maid	Black	M	Mul.	Irregular
Valeria	27	Housewife	Morena/Black	M	White	None
Catarina	27	Teacher	Mul./Black	S	White	3.0
Lorena	28	Maid	Black	S	NA	0.5
Ariana	29	Teacher	Black	M	Black	3.0
Marcelo	29	Unemployed	Mul.	M	Black	Unreported
Carmen	30	Maid	Mul.	S	White	1.0
Adriano	30	Teacher	Mul.	S	White	2.0
Cristiano	31	Ambulance driver	Mul.	M	White	4.0 (two jobs)
Raquel	31	Teacher	White	M	White	3.0
Sonia	32	Teacher	White	S	NA	3.0
Alessandro	33	Pharmacist	White	M	Mul.	5.0–10.0
Tônica	33	Maid	Mul./Black	C	White	0.3
Moema	33	Teacher	White	S	White	5.0
Manoel	33	Farmworker	Black	M	White	Unemployed

Name	Age	Occupation	Color	Marital Status	Color of Partner	Salary
Isabela	34	Business owner	White	M	White	5.0
Rodolpho	35	Doctor	Mul./Black	M	White	22.0
Claudio	37	Dentist	White	S	NA	8.0
Francisco	37	Bus driver	Black	M	Black	5.0
Vera	38	Teacher	White	C	White	1.5–2.0
Rogerio	38	Construction	Black	M	White	3.0
Luisa	40	Housewife	Mul./Black	S	Black	3.0 (boyfriend)
Giovanni	41	Doctor	White	M	White	22.0
Maria	42	Teacher	Mul.	M	White	2.0
Lorenzo	42	Mayor	White	M	White	25.0
Henrique	43	Clerk/Vendor	Mul./Black	M	White	3.0
Mira	45	Housewife	Mul./Black	M	Black	3.0 (husband)
Miguel	45	Teacher/Artist	White	S	White	5.0
Mario	46	Plantation Owner	White	D	White	10.0
Luisa	46	Teacher	Mul./Black	M	White	1.5
Tatiana	51	Housewife	Mul./Black	M	Black	4.0 (husband)
Conceicao	52	Historian	White	M	White	Unknown
Vittorio	52	Military/Poet	White	M	White	1.5
Paulo	54	Electrician	White	M	Black	1.5
Shayla	65	Housewife	Mul.	M	White	Unknown
Joaoquim	66	Farmworker	White	M	Mul.	3.0
Fernando	67	Lawyer/Business owner	Black	D	Black	10.0 owner
Joaquim	67	Retired	Black	M	Mul.	3.0
Snr Arturo	72	Plantation owner	White	M	White	>20.0
Elena	73	Telephone operator	White	W	White	2.0
Albertina	93	Pharmacist	White	W	White	3.0

Note that under the category "Color" if there are two terms separated by a slash, it indicates that a discrepancy existed between how an individual self-identified and how they were identified by others. One word indicates no discrepancy between self-identification and identification by others. Black = Black, Mul. = mulatto, Moreno/a = Moreno/a, and White = White.

Marital status is indicated as follows: S = Single, Unmarried; M = Married; C = Unmarried Domestic Partners; D = Divorced; W = Widowed.

NA = Not applicable (currently has no girlfriend, boyfriend, domestic partner, or spouse

Wages are calculated on the basis of one monthly minimum salary. One monthly minimum salary is the federally mandated minimum wage. At the time that these interviews were conducted (January 1992–1994), one monthly minimum salary was the equivalant of US$75–$80.

NOTES

CHAPTER 1 *Introduction*

1. For a discussion of this in the U.S. press, see Moffett 1996, A1, 6.
2. Translated into English as *The Masters and the Slaves: A Study in the Development of Brazilian Civilization*.
3. See Frazier 1944 as quoted in Hellwig 1992, 123. This essay was originally published under the same title in *Common Sense* 11 (November 1942):363–365. For an excellent discussion of U.S. black perceptions of Brazil, see David Hellwig, "Racial Paradise or Run-Around?: Afro-North American Views of Race Relations in Brazil," *American Studies* 31 (1990):43–60.
4. Several of the volumes produced by scholars funded by the UNESCO research program in the 1950s include: Charles Wagley, *Amazon Town: A Study of Man in the Tropics* (New York: Macmillan, 1952); Roger Bastide and Florestan Fernandes, *Relações raciais entre preto e branco em São Paulo* (São Paulo: Companhia Editora Nacional, 1955); Marvin Harris, *Town and Country in Brazil* (New York: Columbia University Press, 1956); Harry Hutchinson, *Village and Plantation Life in Northeastern Brazil* (Seattle: University of Washington Press, 1957); Fernando Henrique Cardoso and Octávio Ianni, *Côr e mobilidade social em Florianopolis* (São Paulo: Companhia Editora Nacional, 1960).
5. And see, for example, Tony Larry Whitehead and Mary Ellen Conaway, eds., *Self, Sex, and Gender in Cross-Cultural Fieldwork* (Urbana and Chicago: University of Illinois Press, 1986) and Peggy Golde, ed., *Women in the Field: Anthropological Experiences*, 2d ed.(Berkeley and Los Angeles: University of California Press, 1986).

CHAPTER 2 *Vasalia: The Research Site*

1. The Southeast region occupies 10.8 percent of Brazil's land.
2. Vasalia is not the town's actual name. No real names of locations are used.
3. I reviewed records of the history of the region at the office of Fundação Instituto

Brasileiro de Geografica e Estatística (Brazilian Foundation of Geography and Statistics) in the city of Itaperuna.

4. Their descriptions of the conditions under which they lived and worked bore striking similarities to that of pre–civil rights southern United States. See, for example, Dollard 1937 or Powdermaker 1939.

5. I obtained some preliminary unpublished data by visiting the Brazilian Institute of Geography and Statistics. I was unable to obtain any data by race or color because the unpublished preliminary report that I examined did not contain this information. In 1980, the total population of Vasalia was 6,069. The rural population of 4,318 is more than double that of the urban population of 1,751. The size of the rural population is what distinguishes Vasalia from other communities in this region. The rural population is large because of the need for a large coffee plantation labor force, who reside full time on the plantations and farms.

6. The criteria that Brazilians use to assign socioracial identities have been the subject of much discussion (Harris 1964; Sanjek 1971; Telles 1995). There appears to be little consensus on the number and range of categories across regions or communities (Fundação Instituto Brasileiro de Geografia e Estatística—IBGE 1994; 1995). In Vasalia, five commonly terms are used to describe the color of individuals. Terms that denote race are typically avoided in casual conversations. The color terms Vasalians use to self-identify include (1) *branco* (white), (2) *mulatto* (brown/or multiracial), (3) *moreno* (brunet of predominant or exclusive European ancestry/Indian), and (4) *preto/negro* (black- or dark-skinned Afro-Brazilian of no known European ancestry). Residents typically used *moreno* as a polite term and synonym for Afro-Brazilians of all skin colors and physical appearance.

7. The governor of the state of Rio de Janeiro, Leonel Brizola, initiated and implemented a plan that divided the school system into two tiers. Brizola schools had an eight-hour day (instead of the standard four-hour day) and were well financed, well staffed, and open to students on the basis of test scores. These schools targeted more talented and educated students.

8. Until very recently, houses in Vasalia could not be purchased on credit but had to be paid for in full with U.S. currency.

9. This house had been sold by a white middle-class family that had constructed a much larger house several blocks away on a nearby street. Immediately after it was purchased, Helena paid for it to be remodeled and expanded it to almost double the size by the addition of a large kitchen, a fourth bedroom, and an additional living room/television room. The previous small kitchen was converted into a small fourth bedroom that led to the new kitchen.

10. Brazilians discuss and evaluate their income on the basis of the monthly minimum wage, which is set by the federal government. Due to a high rate of inflation, this wage changes every month. In January 1994, the monthly minimum wage was equivalent to approximately US$75 to US$80.

11. Satellite dishes cost approximately US$500, which in 1992 was the equivalent of seven months' salary for an individual who earned the monthly minimum wage. Elementary school teachers earned double or triple the monthly minimum wage.

The high cost of a satellite dish, which had to be purchased with U.S. currency, placed it out of the reach of the overwhelming majority of local residents.

12. This is a small one-room bar frequented primarily by working-class men.

13. Much of the land was only held, not actively farmed, by wealthy whites.

CHAPTER 3 *Mapping the Ideological Terrain*

1. *Criado* is the Brazilian-Portuguese term for both a female servant and a child who has been raised as a servant.

2. For a discussion of the intersection of gender, interracial sexuality, occupational segregation, and perceptions of racism among Afro-Brazilian brothers and sisters, see Twine 1996.

3. Ariana, the darkest-skinned Afro-Brazilian female professional in this community, and not a native Vasalian, was exceptional in pointing to institutions as a place where Afro-Brazilians encountered racism. However, even she did not have a sustained critique that included the concept of institutional racism or proportional representation.

4. On the basis of interviews conducted with a sample of 442 students between the ages of seven and eighteen, Figueira (1990) concluded that racism operates in three arenas (1) among students, (2) among teachers, and (3) in classroom textbooks.

5. Xuxa, born Maria da Graça Meneghel, is a former model and former girlfriend of the legendary black soccer player Pelé. During the time of my research in 1992, her children's show was broadcast six days a week, five hours a day.

6. Although Fernando earned a law degree, he has never practiced as a lawyer. Instead, he operates a small gas station that he purchased from the previous owner.

7. For the complete discussion of this, see Silva and Hasenbalg 1992.

8. Dr. Rodolpho completed his university training in a city in Minas Gerais. He had been born, raised, and educated outside of the state of Rio de Janeiro. Ariana had also been born and raised in Boa Vista and thus was not considered a "real" member of the Vasalian community.

9. See Podesta 1993. Writing about the contradiction between the image of Brazil as a "racial democracy" and the reality of black representation at the federal level, the author noted: "With at least twice the population of the United States, Brazil has 11 black members out of 503 in the lower house of Congress. Only four identify themselves as blacks, and actively take up black issues. There are no black senators or cabinet ministers. No Martin Luther King, Jr. has arisen."

See also "So If It's Black Brazil, Why Is Elite So White?" *The New York Times*, National Edition, Section I, pp. 1, 31. James Brooke writes: "Although 80 percent of Salvador's population is black or of mixed racial descent, the city's Mayor and all but three of the members of the 35 member council are white. On the state level, the racial equation is the same. The Governor of the State of Bahia is white and the congressional delegation looks as if it stepped off a plane from Portugal, Brazil's former colonial power."

CHAPTER 4   *Discourses in Defense*

1. He built the mansion on the main street. The house is ostentatious by rural standards and reflects his wealth and status. Three full-time servants maintain it.
2. In later chapters I discuss this process of white inflation as it operates in national and local memories. See Chapter Seven for a more detailed discussion of the practice of "white inflation" in Vasalia.
3. Also referred to in the literature as *favelas*. This is a poor or working-class community where residents are primarily Afro-Brazilians and other people of color. See the chapter entitled "Deciphering Silence in Morro do Sangue Bom," one section of Robin Sheriff's unpublished dissertation, Anthropology Department, The Graduate Center of the City University of New York.
4. Two years ago, Carla, the daughter of Dona Rosaria, won the beauty contest for morenas. I was shown photos of this contest and learned that a separate beauty contest was held the same year for brancas.
5. Guimarães analyzes 547 articles pertaining to complaints of racial discrimination in twenty Brazilian cities between 1989 and 1994.
6. Datafolha is the name of the survey research branch of this newspaper. See the special supplement to the *Jornal de São Paulo*, Racismo Cordial, published on Sunday, 25 June 1995.

CHAPTER 5   *Embranquecimento*

1. Interviews with eight elementary and high school teachers (11 percent of the local teachers) revealed that television, not newspapers, news magazines, or books, is the primary source of information for teachers. Only one teacher interviewed reported having access to weekly news magazines (because her husband purchased a subscription), which she rarely reads.
2. Until October 1996, there were no magazines in Brazil targeted at Afro-Brazilians. A Brazilian who had lived in the United States for more than seven years returned to Brazil and established *Raca*, the first national magazine dedicated to black Brazilians.
3. Hair relaxer is a product used by U.S. blacks and nonblacks (e.g., South Asians, Italian Americans) to chemically straighten (relax) the hair. There are special products designed for the hair care of black children that were unavailable to Vasalians and difficult to find even in the cities.
4. Although I asked about blacks as a group, she switched to a discussion of black women.
5. She used the Portuguese term *negro*, which signifies black.
6. For another example of white resistance to mestiçagem, see Hammond 1962.
7. Virtually every successful dark-skinned Afro-Brazilian man of any achievement was referred to as Pelé, after the famous soccer player.
8. She describes herself as morena when asked to classify herself racially.
9. See Pierson 1944 for a description of how this process operated in Salvador, Bahia, in the 1930s.

CHAPTER 6   *Memory*

1. In a special issue on "The Black Americas" published by the North American Congress on Latin America (NACLA) in their *Report of the Americas*, the Afro-Brazilian population was estimated to range from 5.9 to 33 percent of the Brazilian population. This range reflects the unreliability of the available census data as an accurate measure of the number of socially recognized black Brazilians.
2. On 1 September 1991, IBASE began a door-to-door campaign visiting, approximately thirty-five million households to collect census data. IBASE also developed and aired television and radio advertisements for this campaign.
3. Abdias do Nascimento lived in political exile in the United States during the most recent Brazilian military dictatorship (1964–1985).
4. Up to now in U.S. court cases, any person with "one drop of African blood" or any known African ancestry is relegated to the black socioracial category.
5. During my fieldwork, I saw no attempts to publicly challenge the registration of a dark-skinned Afro-Brazilian infant as a branco on official documents.
6. For a full discussion of this topic, see the dissertation by Robin Sheriff, 1997. Sheriff asked questions that paralleled those that I asked of residents of Vasalia. Her study is the only other contemporary community study that I identified that specifically examines discourses on race and racism in the city of Rio de Janeiro.
7. More than twenty Afro- and Euro-Brazilians interviewed reported that they had witnessed or been told about this specific social club that denied blacks access to membership and to the events that it sponsored.
8. Robin Sheriff (1997, 18) describes this same practice: "Within this silence is a kind of purposefulness, the involvement of agency, for it is a 'form of forgetting,' or more precisely of 'trying not to remember.'"
9. For a fuller discussion of this, see Stein [1958] 1985, 136–137.
10. Pinturas resemble photographs but are actually realistic drawings that have been painted. These were commonly found in poor and working-class homes. In these drawings, blacks and mulattos were routinely shown with straighter hair and more European features.

CHAPTER 7   *Strategic Responses to Racism*

1. In an analysis of the responses to racism of fifty-eight mixed-race adolescents of African and European descent attending thirty-two different schools in London, Barbara Tizard and Ann Phoenix identified four strategies used to describe what they called "potentially threatening or painful situations." They summarized these strategies as follows: (1) mentally defusing the threat, (2) avoiding or escaping from the threatening situation, (3) tackling the situation directly, and (4) taking steps to prevent or reduce the effects of the threat. These strategies correspond to three of the strategies that Afro-Vasalians used. See Tizard and Phoenix 1993, 132–157.
2. I am employing a modified version of a concept taken from sociologist Edward Telles. In his analysis of racial segregation by residence among Brazilians, Telles

argues that "segregation may also be measured on the dimension of *exposure* or *interaction*. An exposure index measures the extent to which members of a certain group live in the same neighborhood with those of another group. It thus measures the individual experience of segregation" (Telles 1993, 398).

3. For a discussion of the nonperson, see Goffman 1959, 151.

GLOSSARY

botequim Bar. Typically a small one-room or outdoor bar where men congregate.

branco White. Official census term. Terms used in local speech to refer to: (1) light-skinned individuals assumed to be of exclusive or predominant European ancestry, (2) brown-skinned individuals of some known African ancestry who have achieved status or distinction. A very pale blond and/or a foreign-born person from Europe or the United States may be referred to as a *branco branco* (really white).

brincadeira Joke.

carioca Resident of the city of Rio de Janeiro.

criada Female servant. An adopted child who is being raised to serve. A child-servant.

embranquecer To make white. To whiten. To bleach.

embranquecimento The act or effect of whitening.

empregada Female employee. Maid. Domestic servant.

escuro Dark. A polite term for a black or mulatto person.

fazendeiro Farmer. Plantation owner. Rancher.

moreno Brown person. Commonly heard in colloquial speech. An elastic and race-evasive term that is used by whites to refer to brunettes of predominant European and/or indigenous ancestry. This term can be modified by Afro-Brazilians and Euro-Brazilians to include: (1) any brown-skinned and brown-haired individual, (2) dark-haired white Brazilian, (3) sunburnt European, (4) mulattos or blacks (polite term), and (5) individuals of mixed indigenous and European ancestry.

mestiçagem Miscegenation. The mixture of what are presumed to be different races.

mulatto Term heard frequently in colloquial speech to refer to individuals of (1)

salient African ancestry (2) dark-skinned Brazilians of multiracial ancestry, (3) light-skinned Brazilians of any degree of African, Indian, and European ancestry, and (4) dark-skinned Afro-Brazilians or no known mixed
ancestry (polite term).

negro Black person. This term is considered pejorative by some Brazilians and
generally avoided in speech as a term of self-identification. It often appears only in newspapers as a reference to U.S. blacks or African Americans.

pardo Official census term. Not normally heard in speech. A term commonly
found on birth and other legal documents. Synonym for morenos and mulattos. Prior to 1991, this term was an elastic term that included culturally
recognized Brazilian Indians of unmixed ancestry and mixed-race individuals of any degree of African, indigenous and European ancestry.

preconçeito Prejudice. This term is typically used in speech instead of *racismo*
(racism).

preto Black. Polite term for a dark-skinned Afro-Brazilian presumed to be of unmixed African ancestry.

tia Aunt. A term of endearment often used by white elites in a power-evasive
way to refer to their Afro-Brazilian and nonwhite maids and domestic
servants.

BIBLIOGRAPHY

Alvarez, Sonia E. 1990. *Engendering Democracy in Brazil: Women's Movements in Transition Politics*. Princeton: Princeton University Press.

Andrews, George Reid. 1991. *Blacks and Whites in São Paulo, Brazil: 1888–1988*. Madison: University of Wisconsin Press.

Azevedo, Fernando de. 1951. *As elites de côr: Un estudo de Ascensão*. São Paulo: Companhia Editora Nacional.

Bastide, Roger, and Florestan Fernandes. 1955. *Brancos e negros em São Paulo*. São Paulo: Companhia Editora Nacional.

Blauner, Robert. 1972. *Racial Oppression in America*. New York: Harper and Row.

Blee, Kathleen. 1991. *Women of the Klan: Racism and Gender in the 1920s*. Berkeley and Los Angeles: University of California Press.

Bourdieu, Pierre. 1977. *Outline of a Theory of Practice*. Translated by Richard Nice. New York: Cambridge University Press.

Burdick, John. 1995. Brazil's Black Consciousness Movement. In *Fighting for the Soul of Brazil*, ed. Kevin Danaher and Michael Shellenberger. New York: Monthly Review Press.

Cardoso, Fernando Henrique, and Octávio Ianni. 1960. *Côr e mobilidade em Florianópolis*. São Paulo: Companhia Editora Nacional.

Carmichael, Stokely, and Charles Hamilton. 1967. *Black Power: The Politics of Liberation*. New York: Random House.

Carvalho-Neto, Paolo de. 1978. Folklore of the Black Struggle in Latin America. *Latin American Perspectives* 5(2):53–88.

Castro, N. G., and Antonio Sérgio Alfredo Guimarães. 1993. Desigualdades raciais no mercado e nos locais de trabalho. *Estudos Afro-Asiáticos* 24:23–60.

Cunha, Henrique Jr. 1987. A indecisão dos pais face á percepção da discriminação racial na escola pela criança. *Cadernos de Pesquisa* 63:51–53.

Dassin, Joan. 1989. Cultural Policy and Practice in the Nova Republica. *Latin American Research Review* 24(1):115–123.

Degler, Carl. 1971. *Neither Black nor White: Slavery and Race Relations in Brazil and the United States*. New York and London: Macmillan.

Dollard, John. 1937. *Caste and Class in a Southern Town*. New Haven: Yale University Press.

Domingues, Regina. 1988. The Color of a Majority without Citizenship. *Politicas Governmentais* 7(85):14. Rio de Janeiro: Instituto Brasileiro de Análises Sociais e Economicas.

Essed, Philomena. 1991. *Understanding Everyday Racism: Towards an Interdisciplinary Theory*. Newbury Park, Calif. and London: Sage Publications.

Fanon, Frantz. 1967. *Black Skin, White Masks*. New York: Grove Press.

Fernandes, Florestan. 1969. *The Negro in Brazilian Society*. New York: Columbia University Press.

Figueira, Vera Moreira. 1990. O preconceito racial na escola. *Estudos Afro-Asiáticos* 18:63–72.

Folha de São Paulo. 1995. Racismo Cordial (Polite Racism). Special Supplement, Sunday, 25 June.

Fontaine, Pierre-Michel. 1985. *Race, Class, and Power in Brazil*. Berkeley and Los Angeles: University of California Press.

Frankenberg, Ruth. 1993. *White Women, Race Matters: The Social Construction of Whiteness*. Minneapolis: University of Minnesota Press.

Frazier, E. Franklin. 1992 [1944]. Brazil Has No Race Problem. In *African-American Reflections on Brazil's Racial Paradise*, ed. David Hellwig, 121–130. Philadelphia: Temple University Press.

Fredrickson, George. 1981. *White Supremacy: A Comparative Study of American and South African History*. New York and Oxford: Oxford University Press.

Freyre, Gilberto. 1944 [1933]. *The Masters and the Slaves: A Study of the Development of Brazilian Civilization*. New York: Alfred E. Knopf.

Fundação Instituto Brasileiro de Geografia e Estatística—IBGE. 1994. *Brasil em números* 3:1–110. Rio de Janeiro: IBGE.

———. 1995. *Cor da população: Sintese de indicadores 1982–1990*. Rio de Janeiro: IBGE.

Gilliam, Angela. 1988. Telltale Language: Race, Class, and Inequality in Two Latin American Towns. In *Anthropology for the Nineties: Introductory Readings*, ed. Johnnetta Cole, 522–531. Revised and Updated. New York: The Free Press.

———. 1992. From Roxbury to Rio—and Back in a Hurry. In *African-American Reflections on Brazil's Racial Paradise*, ed. David Hellwig, 173–181. Philadelphia: Temple University Press.

Glenn, Evelyn Nakano. 1992. From Servitude to Service Work: Historical Continuities in the Racial Division of Paid Reproductive Labor. *Signs: Journal of Women in Culture and Society* 18(1):1–43.

O Globo. 1992. Racismo mostra a cara nas loja, bares e hoteis da Zona Sul [Racism shows its face in the stores, bars, and hotels of the South Zone]. 1 November.

Goffman, Erving. 1959. *The Presentation of Self in Everyday Life*. New York: Doubleday.

Golde, Peggy. 1970. *Women in the Field: Anthropological Perspectives*. Berkeley and Los Angeles: University of California Press.

Graham, Richard. 1990. *The Idea of Race in Latin America, 1870–1940*. Austin: University of Texas Press.

Guimarães, Antonio Sérgio Alfredo. 1995. Racism and Anti-Racism in Brazil: A Postmodern Perspective. In *Racism and Anti-Racism in World Perspective*, ed. Benjamin Bowser, 208–226. London: Sage Publications.

———. 1996. Racism and the Restriction of Individual Rights: Publicized Racial Discrimination. Paper presented at the 91st Annual Meeting of the American Sociological Association. New York.

Gwaltney, John Langston. 1980. *Drylongso: A Self-Portrait of Black America*. New York: Random House.

Hall, Stuart. 1981. The Whites of Their Eyes: Racist Ideologies and the Media. In *Silver Linings: Some Strategies for the Eighties*, ed. George Bridges and Rosalie Brunt, 28–52. London: Lawrence and Wishart.

———. 1986. Gramsci's Relevance for the Study of Race and Ethnicity. *Journal of Communication Inquiry* 10(2):5–27.

Hammond, Harley. 1962. Race, Social Mobility, and Politics in Brazil. *Race* 6:3–13.

Hanchard, Michael. 1994. *Orpheus and Power: The Movimento Negro of Rio de Janeiro and São Paulo, Brazil, 1945–1988*. Princeton: Princeton University Press.

Harris, Marvin. 1952. Race Relations in Minas Velhas, a Community in the Mountain Region of Central Brazil. In *Race and Class in Rural Brazil*, ed. Charles Wagley, 47–81. Paris: UNESCO.

———. 1964. Racial Identity in Brazil. *Luso-Brazilian Review* 1:21–28.

Hasenbalg, Carlos. 1978. Race Relations in Post-Abolition Brazil: The Smooth Preservation of Racial Inequalities. Ph.D. diss., University of California at Berkeley.

———. 1979. *Discriminação e desigualdades raciais no Brasil*. Rio de Janeiro: Ediçoes Graal.

———. 1983. Anotações sobre a classe média negra no Rio de Janeiro. *Revista de Antropologia* 26:53–59.

———. 1985. Race and Socioeconomic Inequalities in Brazil. In *Race, Class, and Power in Brazil*, ed. Pierce-Michel Fontaine, 25–41. Berkeley and Los Angeles: University of California Press.

———. 1995. Race and Socioeconomic Inequalities in Brazil and Throughout Latin America: Timid Responses to Disguised Racism. In *Constructing Democracy: Human Rights, Citizenship, and Society in Latin America*, ed. Elizabeth Jelin and Eric Hershberg. Boulder: Westview Press.

Hasenbalg, Carlos, and Nelson do Valle Silva. 1990. Raça e oportunidades educacionais no Brasil. *Estudos Afro-Asiáticos* 18:73–92.

Hellwig, David. 1992. *African-American Reflections on Brazil's Racial Paradise*. Philadelphia: Temple University Press.

Heringer, Rosana. 1996. Introduction to the Analysis of Racism and Anti-Racism in Brazil. In *Racism and Anti-Racism in World Perspective*, ed. Benjamin Bowser, 203–207. London: Sage Publications.

Hurston, Zora Neale. [1938] 1990. *Tell My Horse: Voodoo and Life in Haiti and Jamaica*. New Foreword by Ishmael Reed. New York: Harper and Row.

Hutchinson, Harry. 1952. Race Relations in a Rural Community of the Bahian Reconcavo. In *Race and Class in Rural Brazil*, ed. Charles Wagley, 16–46. Paris: UNESCO.

Jackson, Peter. 1987. *Race and Racism: Essays in Social Geography*. London: Allen & Lewin.

Kottak, Conrad. 1990. *Prime-Time Society: An Anthropological Analysis of Television and Culture.* Belmont, Calif.: Wadsworth Publishers.

Landes, Ruth. 1970. A Woman Anthropologist in Brazil. In *Women in the Field: Anthropological Experiences,* ed. Peggy Golde, 119–142. Berkeley and Los Angeles: University of California Press.

Lovell, Peggy. 1987. The Myth of Racial Equality: A Study of Race and Mortality in the Northeast Brazil. *Latinamericanist* 22:1–6.

———. 1989. Income and Racial Inequality in Brazil. Ph.D. diss. University of Florida, Gainesville.

———. 1992. Raça, classe genero e discriminação salarial no Brasil. *Estudos Afro-Asiáticos* 22:85–98.

Lowrie, Samuel. 1939. Racial and National Intermarriage in a Brazilian City. *American Journal of Sociology* 44:684–707.

Margolis, Maxine, and William E. Carter. 1979. *Brazil, Anthropological Perspectives: Essays in Honor of Charles Wagley.* New York: Columbia University Press.

Meade, Teresa, and Gregory Alonso Pirio. 1988. In Search of the Afro-American Eldorado: Attempts by North American Blacks to Enter Brazil in the 1920s. *Luso-Brazilian Review* 25:85–110.

Moffett, Matt. 1996. Seeking Equality: A Racial 'Democracy' Begins the Painful Debate on Affirmative Action. *Wall Street Journal,* 6 August:A1, 5.

Moody, Ann. 1968. *Coming of Age in Mississippi: The Diary of Ann Moody.* New York: Dell Publishing.

Nascimento, Abdias do. [1979] 1989. *Brazil, Mixture or Massacre?: Essays in the Genocide of a Black People.* Dover, Mass.: The Majority Press.

Patai, Daphne. 1988. *Brazilian Women Speak: Contemporary Life Stories.* New Brunswick, N.J.: Rutgers University Press.

Pierson, Donald. 1942. *Negroes in Brazil: A Study of Race Contact at Bahia.* Chicago: University of Chicago Press.

Pinto, Regina Pahim. 1987. A representação do negro em livros didáticos de leitura. *Cadernos de Pesquisa* 63:88–92.

Podesta, Don. 1993. Black Slums Belie Brazil's Self-Image: Equality Is the Law, Inequality Is the Fact. *Washington Post,* 17 August:A12.

Powdermaker, Hortense. 1939. *After Freedom: A Cultural Study of the Deep South.* New York: Viking Press.

Rich, Adrienne. 1979. *On Lies, Secrets, and Silence: Selected Prose, 1966–1978.* New York: W. W. Norton.

Rosemberg, Fúlvia. 1990. Segregação espacial na escola paulista. *Estudos Afro-Asiáticos* 19:97–106.

Sanjek, Roger. 1971. Brazilian Racial Terms: Some Aspects of Their Meaning and Learning. *American Anthropologist* 73 (5):1126–1143.

Schemo, Diana Jean. 1996. "Among Glossy Blondes, A Showcase for Brazil's Black Faces." *New York Times,* 18 Oct., A13.

Scheper-Hughes, Nancy. 1992. *Death without Weeping: The Violence of Everyday Life in Brazil.* Berkeley and Los Angeles: University of California Press.

Schneider, Ronald M. 1991. *Order and Progress: A Political History of Brazil.* Boulder: Westview Press.

Segrest, Mab. 1994. *Memoir of a Race Traitor*. Boston: South End Press.

Sheriff, Robin. 1997. Untitled. Ph.D. diss., Graduate Center of the City University of New York.

Silva, Nelson do Valle. 1985. Updating the Cost of Not Being White in Brazil. In *Race, Class, and Power in Brazil*, ed. Pierre-Michel Fontaine, 42–55. Los Angeles: Center for Afro-American Studies at U.C.L.A.

————. 1987. Distancia social e casamento interracial no Brasil. *Estudos Afro-Asiáticos* 14:54–84.

Silva, Nelson do Valle, and Carlos Hasenbalg. 1992. *Relações raciais no Brasil contemporâneo*. Instituto Universitário de Pesquisas do Rio de Janeiro: Rio Fundo Editora, CEAA.

Simpson, Amelia. 1993. *Xuxa: The Mega-Marketing of Gender, Race, and Modernity*. Philadelphia: Temple University Press.

Skidmore, Thomas. [1974] 1993. *Black into White: Race and Nationality in Brazilian Thought*. New York: Oxford University Press.

————. 1990. Racial Ideas and Social Policy in Brazil, 1870–1940. In *The Idea of Race in Latin America*, ed. Richard Graham, 27. Austin: University of Texas Press.

Stein, Stanley. [1958] 1985. *Vassouras, a Brazilian Coffee County, 1850–1900: The Roles of Planter and Slaves of a Plantation Society*. Princeton: Princeton University Press.

Telles, Edward. 1992. Residential Segregation by Skin Color in Brazil. *American Sociological Review* 57:186–197.

————. 1993. Racial Distance and Region in Marriage: The Case of Marriage among Color Groups. *Latin American Research Review* 28:141–162.

Tizard, Barbara, and Ann Phoenix. 1993. *Black, White, or Mixed-Race: Race and Racism in the Lives of Young People*. London: Routledge.

Toplin, Robert Brent. 1971. *The Abolition of Slavery in Brazil*. New York: Atheneum.

Turner, J. Michael. 1985. Brown into Black: Changing Racial Attitudes of Afro-Brazilian University Students. In *Race, Class and Power in Brazil*, ed. Pierre-Michel Fontaine, 73–94. Los Angeles: Center for Afro-American Studies at U.C.L.A.

Twine, Francine Winddance. 1996. O hiato de genero nas percepções de racismo: O caso dos afro-brasileiros socialmente ascendentes. *Estudos Afro-Asiáticos* 29:37–54.

Wade, Peter. 1993. *Blackness and Race Mixture: The Dynamics of Racial Identity in Colombia*. Baltimore and London: The Johns Hopkins University Press.

Wagley, Charles. 1952. Race and Class in Rural Brazil. Paris: UNESCO.

————. 1979. Introduction. In *Brazil: Anthropological Perspectives: Essays in Honor of Charles Wagley*, ed. Maxine Margolis and William E. Carter, 9. New York: Columbia University Press.

Warren, Jonathan. 1997. Reimagining Indianness: Posttraditional Indians and the Politics of Race in Brazil. Ph.D. diss., University of California at Berkeley.

Webster, Peggy Lovell, and Jeffrey Dwyer. 1988. "The Cost of Being Nonwhite in Brazil." *Sociology and Social Research* 72:136–142.

Wetherell, Margaret, and Jonathan Potter. 1992. *Mapping the Language of Racism: Discourse and the Legitimation of Exploitation*. New York: Columbia University Press.

Willems, Emilio. 1949. Racial Attitudes in Brazil. *American Journal of Sociology* 54:402–408.

Williams, Brackette. 1991. *Stains on My Name, War in My Veins: Guyana and the Politics of Cultural Struggle.* Durham: Duke University Press.

Winant, Howard. 1992. Rethinking Race in Brazil. *Journal of Latin American Studies* 24:173–192.

———. 1994. *Racial Conditions: Politics, Theory, Comparisons.* Minneapolis: University of Minnesota Press.

Wood, Charles. 1988. *The Demography of Inequality in Brazil.* New York: Cambridge University Press.

Wright, Winthrop. 1990. *Café con leche: Race, Class, and National Image in Venezuela.* Austin: University of Texas Press.

INDEX

affirmative action (in Brazil), 1
Alvarez, Sonia, 40
Andrews, George Reid, 9, 44–45, 62, 143, 148–149
anti-racism: Anglo-American elite, 8; black Brazilian activism, 2, 4, 62; Brazilian legislation, 3

bahianos (Northeasterners), 16
Barbosa, Rui, 111
beauty, hierarchy of, 88–93
black movement (*movimento negro*), 2
black professionals, 11, 102, 141–152
Blauner, Robert, 61
Blee, Kathleen, 100
Bourdieu, Pierre, 66
brancos (whites), 19
Burdick, John, 2

Cardoso, Fernando Henrique, 4
Carmichael, Stokely, and Charles Hamilton, 61
Carnival, 128
Carvalho-Neto, Paolo, 4
Catholic Church, and racial discrimination, 29–30
census: Brazilian, 15, Rio de Janeiro, 15
children: and access to anti-racist education, 152–153; adoption of, 35–38
class inequality; 7, 67–73

class mobility, 105
coffee, 16–17, 26–27
common sense, 3, 56, 66
criacao (adoption), 35–38
Cunha, Henrique, Jr., 4

Dassin, Joan, 111
Degler, Carl, 37
discourses: of class inequality, 67; of containment, 78–85; of cultural inferiority, 77–78; demographic, 74–76
Dollard, John, 33–34, 100, 104
Domingues, Regina, 112–113
doxa (Bourdieu's term), 66–67
Dwyer, Jeffrey, 4

education: exclusion of Afro-Brazilians from school textbooks, 55; racial disparities in higher education, 58–60;
embranquecimento (whitening), 87–109; in birth registration, 114–115; in census records, 112–113; in family genealogies, 122–127; family photo albums, 129–132
empregada domestica, 38
Espirito Santo, 17
Essed, Philomena, 140, 153

Fanon, Frantz, 87

About the Author

France Winddance Twine is a professor of sociology at Duke University and the University of California at Santa Barbara. She earned her Ph.D. from the University of California at Berkeley. Her articles on racial consciousness, racial identity formations, and antiracism have been published in English and Portuguese in international and interdisciplinary journals in Brazil, Europe, and the United States. She has been an editor of four volumes and is a member of the editorial boards of *Sociological Theory* and *Ethnic and Racial Studies*. Her forthcoming book is titled *Bearing Blackness in Britain*. France Winddance Twine was born and raised in Chicago, Illinois.